The
Trout Point Lodge
Cookbook

The
Trout Point Lodge
Cookbook

Creole Cuisine from New Orleans to Nova Scotia

Daniel Abel, Charles Leary, and Vaughn Perret

Photographs by Wayne Barrett

Foreword by John Besh

RANDOM HOUSE CANADA

www.randomhouse.ca

Library and Archives of Canada Cataloguing in Publication

Abel, Daniel G.
The Trout Point Lodge cookbook : Creole cuisine from New Orleans
to Nova Scotia / Daniel Abel, Charles Leary, Vaughn Perret ; photographs by Wayne Barrett.

Includes index.
ISBN 0-679-31247-1

1. Trout Point Lodge. 2. Cookery, Creole. 3. Cookery, American—Louisiana style.
4. Cookery—Nova Scotia. I. Leary, Charles Leland II. Perret, Vaughn J. III. Title.

TX715.A138 2004a
641.59763   C2004-903311-5

Printed and bound in Hong Kong on acid-free paper

2 4 6 8 9 7 5 3 1

First Edition

DESIGN BY MERCEDES EVERETT

To our families
and
our Creole-Acadian heritage

Foreword

In the early 1990s, when I came home to southern Louisiana after years of culinary training around the globe, I had the pleasure of meeting Danny, Charlie, and Vaughn, who, as organic farmers, wild food harvesters, and cheese makers, shared my newly resolved goals of working with a more regional style of cooking. It was through my pilgrimages to their Chicory Farm in the countryside north of New Orleans that I was inspired to work toward perfecting a truly localized cuisine, based on sustainable foods from small farms. All three of these authors possess a contagious love for the land, for its cultivation, and for producing exceptional food. They have continued to expand upon their earlier successes at Trout Point Lodge, set in the Acadian homeland of Nova Scotia, and this book distills the fruits of over fourteen years of farming and cooking.

Years of shared bottles of wine and artisanal cheeses later, I'm still inspired by their simple and heartfelt approach to Creole food. The depth of Vaughn and Charlie's knowledge about indigenous foods and about the age-old methods of growing, producing, and using such foods has helped my cooking continue to evolve to this day at my restaurants in New Orleans, where I exercise many lessons learned from these two. Danny and his love of life and great food inspire me to enjoy what I do. *The Trout Point Lodge Cookbook* isn't just a cookbook—it truly exemplifies the way we should all try to cook, eat, and live, through a respect for our food, how it is prepared, and where it comes from.

JOHN BESH,
chef and partner of
Restaurant August,
The Besh Steakhouse, and
Cîté bar and brasserie,
New Orleans

Preface

Friends and Trout Point Lodge guests seem to be intrigued by our story: we are three professionals who diverted from established careers as lawyers and professors to pursue a love of food and cooking. At the outset, we could have never imagined that we would become chefs, farmers, gardeners, cheese makers, or cookbook authors. Undoubtedly we would have accomplished none of this without the inspiring influence of the Creole French and Spanish culture of southern Louisiana.

This is our story:

By the mid-1980s, two of us, Vaughn Perret and Daniel Abel, had known each other for decades, having met while working for a political campaign in New Orleans. Danny grew up in the heart of Cajun country, Lafayette, and worked in local restaurants during high school and college. In places like Thelma's of Breaux Bridge, he discovered a love for cooking and perfected essential techniques of authentic Cajun cookery that he still draws on today. After graduating from university, he studied and worked in Italy, Mexico, and many other places around the world. He then moved out of the Cajun heartland to New Orleans, and among other things, managed jazz musician Al Hirt's Café St. Cécile. Along the way, he also pursued degrees in English literature and law. As a lawyer, Danny worked on some of the nation's biggest legal cases, moving at one point to Puerto Rico for five years and later coauthoring a book on gun violence and children. But throughout his career, Danny never lost his love for food and cooking.

Danny's friend Vaughn, a New Orleans native, attended Loyola and Tulane

universities, receiving degrees in history and meso-American cultural anthropology, and then, like Danny, headed to law school. Having spent most of his life in the Crescent City, Vaughn decided that for law school he wanted to explore other parts of the United States, so he went to Cornell University in Ithaca, New York. Ithaca supported an excellent farmers' market and an abundance of independent market gardeners, wineries, cheese makers, and excellent restaurants, and he had no trouble taking full advantage of its culinary allures.

Having grown up in Louisiana, where family get-togethers often brought twenty or more people to the table for a Creole feast, Vaughn appreciated traditional styles of food and cooking. He also was very familiar with gardening and farming, having passed many hours at his grandmother's house, tending her greenhouse, garden, and collection of ducks, chickens, and geese at her veritable mini-farm on St. Charles Avenue, in the middle of uptown New Orleans. At home he helped his father care for the family vegetable garden; ventured out to the local bayous to fish; gathered crawfish and crabs; and harvested figs and pears, as well as other fruits and berries from abandoned homesteads in the local woods.

Vaughn spent time during college and graduate school in one of the world's culinary capitals, Paris, honing his palate and appreciation for good food. He also spent one summer in legal training in another culinary wonderland: Shanghai, China.

Born in Oregon, Charles spent his early years on the West Coast, high school in Colorado, college in Ohio, and substantial time in China, Taiwan, and Hong Kong. He had grown up with a love of farming, animals, and travel, a curious combination that he put aside for graduate studies in Chinese history. Charles

and Vaughn met when Vaughn saw Charles reading a Chinese document in one of Cornell University's dining halls and struck up a conversation. They both befriended Jane North, a woman who sold cheese at the Ithaca farmers' market. Not just any cheese, this kind was made from sheep's milk, an unusual dairy product in the United States in the mid-1980s. Jane and her husband, Karl, it turned out, had lived for years in France, where they learned about farmstead cheese production.

When Danny came to Ithaca to visit, the three of us went to see Jane and Karl. We tasted their cheeses and surveyed the farm and creamery in nearby Marathon, New York. Their efforts were proof that French farming styles and foodways could be successfully transplanted to the New World, and this idea inspired us to one day pursue farming and cheese making ourselves—we dreamed of actually making the foods we had grown up loving.

The realities of making a living and pursuing our various careers delayed our plans for a short time. While Vaughn went to work for a Park Avenue law firm in Manhattan, Danny continued his law practice in New Orleans, and Charles attended classes and completed his doctorate at Cornell. In 1990, having kept in close contact, we decided to meet up in New Orleans. Charles taught on the adjunct faculty at Tulane University while writing his dissertation, and Vaughn and Danny continued practicing law. It wasn't long before we pooled our resources and decided to look for a farm, driving up and down the highways and roads north of New Orleans in what is known as the "Florida Parishes," an area that had once been the independent Republic of Florida, and before that part of the Spanish colonial empire.

Before World War II, Louisiana had been a part-French, part-Spanish cultural enclave within the southern United States, with its own distinctive farm products, native livestock, homemade cheeses, and cooking techniques. (France had ruled Louisiana from 1698 to 1763, and Spain from 1763 to 1803, and both countries left a deep impression in language, architecture, and style of food preparation.) But since the 1950s, with more exposure to other markets and

changes in consumer habits, southern Louisiana had lost much of its distinctive French and Spanish food heritage.

Creole Cream Cheese, for example, was a native Louisiana fresh cheese made for centuries in homes and small dairies around New Orleans. By the mid-1990s, all but one tiny Creole Cream Cheese manufacturer had closed its doors, and not many people made cheese at home anymore. Likewise, the long-standing tradition of gathering wild foods—venturing out into the swamps, bayous, and forests to find edible wild mushrooms and plants—had disappeared with the advent of larger urban areas and a more fast-paced existence, even in the so-called Big Easy.

Therefore, when we looked around the culinary landscape of New Orleans in the early nineties, stopping by restaurants and the centuries-old French Market, we saw none of the indigenous southern Louisiana products—homemade aged cheeses, wild-harvested plants and mushrooms, and traditional Louisiana vegetables—that had at one time been such an important part of what made Creole cooking special. We wanted to contribute to and enhance the kind of fresh, local ingredients available to restaurants and in the food markets. We also believed in local, technologically appropriate, and sustainable agriculture, and knew that many chefs had come to appreciate the same concepts. We believed that if freshly picked lettuces, cheeses made with local milk, and wild foods harvested from the forests and swamps of Louisiana were offered to area chefs, they would jump at the opportunity to use these products on their menus.

With a little cash and a big mortgage, we bought a hundred-acre wooded parcel with a small brick house on the premises, an hour and a half north of New Orleans in a farming community called Mount Hermon, where we were determined to grow vegetables, cultivate mushrooms, collect wild foods, raise goats, cows, and sheep, and make cheese. We set about farming with sustainability, organics, and diversity of production as our goals, avoiding the common, modern practice of monocultural farming. We taught ourselves through reading and experimentation, drawing on our travels and experiences to guide our efforts. It was not easy, and we all pursued other jobs to make the farming life a financial reality during the first couple of years.

We named our place "Chicory Farm," after the indigenous Louisiana plant, and populated it with purebred Nubian and LaMancha goats, Louisiana Native and East Friesian sheep, chickens, and guinea fowl. We also started extensive market garden plantings and built a creamery, a barn, and a mushroom laboratory. We began by selling our handmade, European-style cheeses and exotic produce every weekend at the French Market, the traditional food market along the Mississippi River, and started introducing our products to skeptical restaurateurs. Soon we were selling ten different kinds of goat and cow's milk cheeses to the venerable Commander's Palace and the then-new restaurant Emeril's. Just as we had hoped, Chicory Farm proved what the New Orleans food community sought, though this often meant we had to politely educate chefs and sous-chefs about cooking and eating things that they had never imagined could be edible. We remember instructing Emeril Lagasse's kitchen staff about the virtues of what to them must have looked like bizarre, mold-covered cheeses; trying to convince Jamie Shannon's sous-chefs in the Commander's Palace kitchen to accept his order of giant puffballs and other strange-looking fungi; and catching Larry Forgione's attention with the most pungent of all American cheeses, a washed-rind beauty we called "Catahoula" (the smell remained with him while driving home, inspiring him to invent new ways of using it on his menu at An American Place in New York).

We named the Chicory Farm cheeses after the Louisiana parishes (the state doesn't have counties): Catahoula, St. John, De Soto, Washington, Iberia, and Orleans, among others. Each featured a different kind of production method and aging, or *affinage,* using the native Louisiana molds and bacteria to form rinds and ripen the cheese from the outside, as had been done for centuries in France. Chicory Farm cheeses and their distinctive *affinage* drew the attention of Europeans, resulting in our induction into the French Cheesemaker's Guild in 1994. Soon other restaurants, from Brigsten's and Bella Luna to Artesia and the Grill Room, featured Chicory Farm products. The word spread, and before long, wheels of Catahoula and Orleans could be found in New York, Chicago, and San Francisco. The likes of Eric Ripert, Joho, and Gary Danko put them on menus, while Dean & DeLuca, Fairway Market, Zabar's, and Oakville Grocery sold them to a public warming up to the new kinds of American cheese. However, without the enthusiastic support and encouragement of New Orleans's chefs, Chicory Farm might never have succeeded.

Chicory Farm received organic certification and expanded to grow tender baby lettuces, beans, edible flowers, and peppers. Vaughn cloned and cultivated wild edible mushrooms, and also collected wild fungi, delivering giant puffballs, lion's manes, exotic milky caps, chicken-of-the-woods, chiodini, and savory chanterelles to favorite restaurant customers. By 1996 the farm had won a na-

tional honor from the Small Business Administration: the first annual Tibbetts Award. When the Crescent City Farmer's Market opened, Chicory Farm enthusiastically supported the effort, selling organic salad mixes, wild and cultivated mushrooms, and hundreds of pounds of cheese to New Orleaneans. Likewise, when Baton Rouge residents opened their Red Stick Farmer's Market, Chicory Farm was there from the beginning. In just a few years the goal we had dreamed of—a renaissance in small farms and local produce in south Louisiana—had become a reality.

In 1995, five years after buying the property in Mount Hermon, Vaughn's mother, Laura, joined us in our decision to open our own restaurant, the Chicory Farm Café, a place that would truly showcase all of Chicory Farm's products in the Creole style of cuisine native to New Orleans. Located uptown near Tulane and Loyola universities, Chicory Farm Café received excellent reviews and national attention. What made the café unique was the fact that it featured Creole *vegetarian* cuisine, an accomplishment that was not easy to come by in a meat-loving city like the Big Easy.

We were always searching for new projects, and our interest in the European cultural heritage of North America was piqued during a visit to Nova Scotia in the summer of 1996. This trip sparked a new idea: a center that provided cooking lessons, where people could actually come and take a culinary vacation of sorts. The Acadian connection with Louisiana had drawn us to Nova Scotia, and we purchased land in Yarmouth County, home in the eighteenth century to one of the largest Acadian populations in historical Acadie. In 1998 we decided to sell our Louisiana businesses and move our entrepreneurial talents to the ancient Acadian homeland. Though it was difficult to leave the supportive Louisiana food community, in Nova Scotia we saw potential for creativity, with abundant natural food resources and an ideal summer and fall climate.

The result was La Ferme d'Acadie, a creamery, and Trout Point Lodge, an inn and cooking school located in the Tobeatic Wilderness. Now, hundreds of people journey to southwestern Nova Scotia to simply relax at the Lodge or to take a cooking lesson with us. They learn about the French and Spanish culinary heritage of the Americas, see what "fresh" seafood really means, and go out into the woods or onto the salt marshes to forage and collect for their supper.

Trout Point is both the Lodge and a private nature preserve enveloping two hundred acres of Acadian forest, surrounded by the confluence of the Tusket and Napier rivers. We designed and built a massive log and stone Great Lodge, made of Atlantic Canadian spruce and blue Nova Scotia granite. It houses elegant guest rooms, a great room and library, the dining room and kitchen, and also contains eight stone fireplaces, a wood-fired oven, and numerous breezeways, patios, and porches for our guests' enjoyment. The haute rustic interior, composed of log-and-twig furniture we designed and had produced in the local French village of Wedgeport, evokes the great lodges of New York's Adirondacks as well as Yarmouth County's own tradition of hunting camps, dating from the days when the area was a favored summer vacation spot for figures like Franklin D. Roosevelt, Babe Ruth, and Zane Grey.

While we prepare a changing daily menu for breakfast, lunch, and dinner, our guests canoe or kayak, swim the pristine waters of the Tusket River, hike into the verdant forests of the wilderness area, or simply relax without the usual interferences and tensions of the outside world.

First and foremost as farmers and food producers, we approach cooking from an angle that emphasizes the importance of high-quality basic ingredients, and we still carry out our beliefs in small-scale, local, and sustainable agriculture. We grow vegetables, lettuces, and herbs in an organic garden that expands every year. We purchase additional produce from local farmers. We use only freshly caught seafood brought to the docks at Yarmouth, and we make sustainable use of the bounty in surrounding forests and marshes.

We prepare the food at Trout Point with Creole style, which is derived from our New Orleans roots. Like the food of New Orleans, our dishes represent a combination of the elevated and the rustic, the simple and the flavorful, whose beauty lies not in its sculptural qualities, complexity of preparation, or use of exotic ingredients, but rather in its straightforward expression of what we believe tastes good combined with a heartfelt effort to use local, fresh, and self-gathered or -grown ingredients. Trout Point's recipes are easy for home cooks to prepare, and we hope that the recipes we share here will be used time and again.

Acknowledgments

It would be impossible to properly thank everyone who contributed in some way to the creation of this book, starting with the staff of Chicory Farm and the Chicory Farm Café in Louisiana, and including everyone who has worked to make Trout Point Lodge such a success, especially Ronnie Harris and Joyce Harlow. We want to thank Jo Fagan, Stacey Glick, Mary Bahr, and especially Laura Ford for helping at different stages to bring the book to publication. Shelley Berg, Katherine Ness, Shauna Toh, and Jude Grant at Random House should be singled out for excellence. John Besh deserves praise for his gracious words. Thanks to Cyrille LeBlanc and the Tusket River Project for information about the Tobeatic Wilderness. Darcy Belisle assisted with the Wild Foods chapter during the summer of 2003, and Guillermo Escamilla was indispensable while preparing dishes for photography. We could not have had a better photographer and friend than Wayne Barrett.

Contents

We have spent years learning the edible wild foods of North America, and it is critically important that novices do not collect wild plants or mushrooms without having expert guidance. We recommend consulting books on wild edible plants and mushrooms and also joining a local mycological society before attempting to collect any of the wild plants or mushrooms listed in this book. In addition, before collecting on public or private lands, always check with state authorities regarding regulations of wild plant harvesting, as there may be areas where picking is not allowed. And always receive permission from private land owners before harvesting plants and mushrooms on their land.

Introduction

New World Creole from
New Orleans to Nova Scotia

In 1605, French explorer Samuel de Champlain discovered and named Cape Forchu, befriending Mi'kmaq natives dwelling in the southernmost part of the Nova Scotia peninsula, where Trout Point Lodge now stands. The next year, after Champlain and his fellow adventurers claimed Nouvelle France—present-day Nova Scotia—for the French Crown, they founded the New World's first culinary society, l'Ordre de Bon Temps (the Order of Good Cheer), at Port Royal on the vast Bay of Fundy. The elaborate meals prepared by the Order raised the spirits and the culinary standards of Port Royal residents during the dismal winter of 1606–07. These uplifting feasts commenced the tradition of New World Creole cuisine in North America, with Champlain and his cohorts applying European know-how and *joie de vivre* to local cooking and ingredients. Later French settlers, known as the Acadians, carried on the Order's culinary traditions in a territory then known as Acadie until they were expelled from their lands in the 1750s.

The French settlers established homes in Acadie, covering what is contemporary Nova Scotia and beyond. The Acadians had good relations with the Mi'kmaq natives, and they set to farming and fishing along the Bay of Fundy in a land they found hospitable, peaceful, and naturally rich. So successful were the Acadians in their pursuit of producing good food that by the early seventeenth century they had started exporting vegetables and grains across the Gulf of Maine to New

England, as well as salt cod to Europe. The waters from Acadie to Newfoundland proved to be one of the world's best fishing grounds, supplying cod for the Mediterranean trade in addition to a wealth of other seafood. North American cod—dried, salted, and known throughout the world as *bacalao*—soon ended up in the food markets of France, Italy, Portugal, Spain, and North Africa.

Marc Lescarbot, an educated and cultured man of Paris and a colleague of Champlain, described the wonders of la Nouvelle France, focusing, as one might expect, on its culinary customs. In his 1609 book, *History of New France,* he describes in loving detail the abundance and diversity of New World foods, including not only his own experience in Canada, but also that of explorers in the French settlements in Florida and Brazil, showing how extensively French culture reached into the Americas. Describing the shifting responsibility amongst the Order's members for a day's meals, Lescarbot evokes the Rue aux Ours (Street of the Bears) near Paris's celebrated Les Halles food markets, home of numerous food vendors and the birthplace of formal culinary apprenticeship in France:

> This person had the duty of taking care that all around the table were well and honorably provided for. This was so well carried out that, though the epicures of Paris often tell us that we had no Rue aux Ours over there, as a rule we made as good cheer as we could have in this same Rue aux Ours and at less cost. For there was no one who, two days before his turn came, failed to go hunting or fishing, and to bring back some delicacy in addition to our ordinary fare. So well was this carried out that never at breakfast did we lack some savory meat of flesh or fish, and still less at our midday or evening meals; for that was our chief banquet.

Here Lescarbot is expressing the essence of Creole cooking. He writes of the importance of the social enjoyment of food, of the well-developed cooking techniques and high culinary standards of mother Europe, and of bringing back some native ingredients and delicacies to the table to enrich the meal. Lescarbot and Champlain had started something new with the feasts of 1606–07, and we embody those same practices at Trout Point.

Nova Scotia thus was the birthplace of the Creole culinary tradition that eventually spread to Louisiana, the Gulf Coast, and the Caribbean before becoming famous all over the world. Originating in New France and in Acadie, Creole cuisine and culture grew into its own distinctive entity, blending Spanish, French, and Afro-Caribbean elements. Although the French influence predominated in Nova Scotia, as it does today, trade routes brought direct commerce with Caribbean ports and other southern climes. Louisiana's Creole food still reflects a blending of French and Spanish cooking techniques combined with Afro-Caribbean and North American ingredients.

Even after France lost her North American territories to the British, the Acadians remained in what the victors renamed "New Scotland." When anti-French sentiment swelled in the 1750s, the British expelled the French Acadians from their homeland. Some eventually returned to Nova Scotia as second-class citizens, while many others settled in places like the Caribbean islands and southern Louisiana, where the contemporary Spanish rulers of the Louisiana colony welcomed new inhabitants. Here families with names like LeBlanc, Comeau, Boudreau, and Doucette became today's Cajuns, often marrying with French Creoles from New Orleans and thus literally blending Acadian and Creole cultures.

The heart and soul of Champlain's Order of Good Cheer, where food and drink raised the human spirit in its New World environment, lives on in Louisiana to this day. This enjoyment and refinement of the good life is precisely why so many people from around the world journey to New Orleans and southern Louisiana to vacation, relax, and, most importantly for many, to eat.

We went in the opposite direction.

After establishing a farm, foods business, and restaurant in Louisiana, we decided to see what had become of ancient Acadie. The results of that ongoing journey lie inside this cookbook. The spirit, recipes, techniques, and discussions found here are built upon the foundation first established by Champlain and the others who founded the Order of Good Cheer four centuries ago. We inherited this tradition—how we think about food and how it should be cooked—directly from the earliest French explorers. We have also explored the range of Creole cooking and foodways, from Louisiana to Canada, from the Mediterranean to the Caribbean, and from the farmer's field to the delicacies of woods, marsh, and bayou.

Creole, Cajun, and Acadian

In southern Louisiana there exist, though perhaps in quickly vanishing states, two separate styles of cooking: Creole and Cajun. Paul Prudhomme effectively joined the two styles in his first cookbook, *Chef Prudhomme's Louisiana Kitchen*, published in 1984. His book combines his culinary upbringing in Cajun Opelousas with his considerable time cooking in the New Orleans Creole kitchen of Ella Brennan's Commander's Palace restaurant, and his cooking created a renaissance of interest in French New World styles that has lasted to this day.

Creole is the cooking of urban and urbane New Orleans. It is more refined than Cajun fare, and uses more tomato-based sauces, French technique, Spanish Mediterranean sensibilities, Afro-Caribbean ingredients, a complex range of herbs and spices, and sophisticated restaurant know-how in its preparations. New Orleans was a major commercial port, and its economic importance and cosmopolitan character made it different from the rural Cajun areas. Creole remains tied historically to the colonization of new territories, and to the new kinds of social and political elites that evolved in urban areas, mixing and blending both peoples and cuisines from different areas to produce something new, distinct, and refined.

Cajun and Acadian styles of cooking, on the other hand, have rural roots, and to this day both Cajun and Acadian communities are primarily small coastal settlements. The cooking is simple and unpretentious, designed to nourish and to adapt readily to a variety of ingredients that are grown, hunted, fished, or gathered. Louisiana's Cajuns generally escaped the domination of English or other colonial overlords, and thus retained their French culture, language, and cooking traditions. The Acadians in Nova Scotia, by contrast, suffered under the cultural domination and discrimination of Anglo-Canadian authority. Although they attempted to hold on to their distinct cultural identity, they lost their ability to farm, and with that some of the diversity of their food traditions. The Acadians, however, are the quintessential fishermen, and they bring to shore the world's finest and freshest seafood: lobster, cod, haddock, scallops, tuna, and a variety of other *fruits de mer.*

The food of Trout Point Lodge relies upon the richness and abundance of New World ingredients coupled with a continental European appreciation for technique, seasoning, and the senses. Cooking for the senses produces food that not only tastes good but also is attractive in color and appearance, texture, and smell, exciting all of the human appetite. Such cooking was preserved in these different French cultural outposts.

This book's focus is on seafood and vegetable-based dishes, an emphasis that comes from the historical and agricultural context of both Louisiana and Nova Scotia, two environments where fishing, the harvesting of wild foods, and gardening defined the scope of many meals. As William Kaufman and Sister Mary Ursula Cooper wrote in their 1962 book, *The Art of Creole Cookery,* "No resources are overlooked, and Creole cooks even today search for wild greens from field, stream, and woods to add an unusual touch."

At Trout Point Lodge, we serve fixed lunch and dinner menus to our seasonal summer and fall guests, and we teach Creole cooking techniques to those who come to the Nova Scotia Seafood Cooking School. The Lodge lies within the Tobeatic Wilderness Preserve, along the banks of the Tusket and Napier rivers in Argyle Municipality, the province's largest French-speaking Acadian community. For three years we also operated a farm and creamery on Chebogue Point, the historical site of one of the largest Acadian settlements and farming communities before their expulsion in the 1750s. The name Chebogue is an Acadian French phonetic transliteration of a Mi'kmaq word for the area describing its vast marshlands and tidal rivers, places the Acadians diked, drained, and farmed. Chebogue continues to offer rich soils for growing as well as the world's best fishing grounds. The Chebogue salt marsh supports abundant wild treasures, as do the inland forests of the Tobeatic—home to black trumpet, chanterelle, and cèpe mushrooms, wild greens, cucumber root, wintergreen, sweet fern, native blueberries, and fiddlehead ferns. Recipes using many of these wild foods can be found in Chapter 3.

The protected 386 square miles of the Tobeatic Wilderness immediately surrounding Trout Point Lodge is the last truly wild area in Nova Scotia and the largest protected wilderness in Atlantic Canada. The headwaters of the East Branch, which flow by the Great Lodge, lie a canoe portage away from the Shelburne River, the most remote river in Nova Scotia. This Canadian Heritage River links the Tusket watershed with Kejimkujik National Park.

Guests at the Lodge often arrive complaining about how remote and hard-to-find we are. But in a short time they relax, forget the cares of the outside world, and begin to appreciate what it is that surrounds them. The main Tusket River flows north to south, dividing the basin into western and eastern sections. The upper East Branch and the Napier rivers, which flow together at Trout Point, drain an extensive plateau at around four hundred feet above sea level. Known as the Granite Barrens, this area is part of the "Empty Quarter," and devoid of people. The extensive granite bedrock has only a thin cover of loose, stony till soil, through which beautiful pine, spruce, and hardwood trees eke out their existence, turned and twisted into beautiful shapes. The glaciers of the last Ice Age left huge granite boulders strewn about the landscape surrounding the Lodge. A hike into the Tobeatic Wilderness from Trout Point reveals numerous streams flowing between shallow, irregular lakes, bogs, swamps, and swales. Some area lakes boast beaches of white granite sand. The glaciers also created long promi-

nent eskers—huge linear tracts of sand—that are said to be the longest in the Maritimes.

We have cleared a place in these environs to cultivate a vegetable garden, and as at Port Royal in 1606, we bake our bread in a brick oven fired by wood hewn from the surrounding forest. Four hundred years after Champlain, we, transplants from another former French colony, continue the tradition started with the Order of Good Cheer by using local fresh ingredients, fish just plucked from nearby waters, and the inspiring abundance of wild foods.

Insulated and inspired by this magical and beautiful natural environment, each day we pursue a re-creation of the *bon temps* enjoyed four centuries ago. In this book, we have adapted some standard Louisiana dishes, like gumbo and jambalaya, to new ingredients, like salmon or smoked haddock, and have likewise taken some Acadian specialties, like Pâté à la Rapure or blueberry tart, and given them new seasonings. The reader will also find French culinary techniques applied to New World ingredients in the creation of new dishes, and some historical recipes culled from our researches into Acadian, Creole, and Cajun foodways or from our childhood memories.

As we say in Louisiana, *Laissez les bon temps roulez!*

The
Trout Point Lodge
Cookbook

Chapter one

Appetizers

They employ their free time by going to collect Mussels that are under the ocean in great quantities just in front of the Fort, or the Lobster (a species of crayfish), or Crabs, which are abundant under the rocks at Port Royal, or the Cockles that lie beneath the silt of all the rivers of this Port. All these are taken without nets and without boats. . . . Of bread, no one goes wanting, and each one has three cups of wine, pure and fine.

Marc Lescarbot, *Histoire de la Nouvelle-France,* 1609

In the Creole tradition, a proper home meal consists of three distinct stages, each of which may have several courses or dishes, rather than the more typical North American model of one plate with three or four different foods on it. These stages and courses give tempo and variety to a meal. Serving several courses doesn't necessarily mean that the cook has to spend more time in the kitchen or create a meal so complex that he or she feels tied to the stove. It simply means a little more planning, resulting in a more leisurely dining experience.

Perhaps more than other courses, appetizers offer the opportunity for creativity: These small plates allow us to use the freshest ingredients, to construct an interesting combination of flavors, or to bring forth a single unforgettable item, like fresh asparagus, succulent fennel, or scallops just off the boat.

The traditional home meal consists of a first stage (hors d'oeuvres and/or soups), a second stage (fish, meats, savory and sweet vegetable dishes, and salads), and the third stage (sweets, fruits, nuts, desserts, and candies). After-dinner drinks follow. At Trout Point, guests receive a leisurely service of separate stages in the Creole style, giving them time to relax and enjoy their meal times with us.

Wild Mushroom Pâté

½ cup extra virgin olive oil

7 cups cleaned and coarsely chopped mixed fresh wild mushrooms, or a combination of wild and domestic (chanterelles, portobellos, shiitakes, oysters, cremini, porcini, and/or morels)

¼ cup finely chopped scallions (white and green parts) or shallots

¾ cup sweet dessert wine, such as a Muscat

½ teaspoon salt

¼ teaspoon freshly ground black pepper

1 cup heavy cream

5 egg yolks

2 tablespoons cornstarch

2 teaspoons chopped fresh chives

The Cajuns and the Acadians share a common tradition of collecting wild mushrooms, as we can attest from forays in both the Nova Scotia boreal forests and the swamps of Honey Island, Louisiana. We enjoy picking golden chanterelles and black trumpets in the Acadian woods surrounding the Lodge just as much as we enjoyed gathering them back in Louisiana. (The great Creole chefs of New Orleans rarely if ever ventured out to the swamps themselves, but they sure treasured what we carried back to them from the domain of water moccasins, copperheads, and alligators!)

This dish puts such hard-gained treasures to good use, featuring the complex, deep, earthy flavors of wild mushrooms. If you don't have enough of the wild varieties, just mix in some domestic white button or portobello mushrooms.

Cleaning Mushrooms

When preparing mushrooms, don't wet them if they're dirty; simply brush them off using your hands or, if necessary, a small soft-bristle brush. If you're dealing with meaty, mature wild specimens like porcini (which the French call *cèpes* and the scientists call *Boletus edulis*), it's advisable to cut them in half to check for worms.

1. Preheat the oven to 350° F. Grease a standard loaf pan or terrine well with oil or butter and set it aside.
2. Heat the olive oil in a large skillet over medium heat. Add the mushrooms and scallions,

and sauté until the mushrooms soften and the scallions become translucent, about 5 minutes. Set aside.

3. Pour the wine into a small saucepan and simmer over low heat until reduced to 2 tablespoons, about 15 minutes. Set aside.

4. Spoon half the mushroom/onion mixture into a blender or food processor. Add the reduced wine, the salt, and the pepper. Puree. Then, with the machine running, slowly add the cream and the egg yolks. When the mixture is thoroughly blended and smooth, transfer it to a bowl. Sift in the cornstarch, stirring to ensure that no lumps form. Stir in the remaining mushroom/onion mixture.

5. Transfer the mixture to the prepared terrine, spreading it evenly and firmly with a rubber spatula.

6. Place the terrine in a baking dish or casserole, and pour in enough water to reach halfway up the sides of the terrine. Bake for about 1 hour, or until an inserted wooden skewer comes out clean. Remove the terrine from the water bath and allow to cool for 1 hour. Unmold the terrine onto a serving plate. Cover, and refrigerate the terrine for at least 2 hours. Sprinkle with the chives before serving. The terrine will keep up to 1 week in the refrigerator.

Grilled Oyster Mushrooms and Garlic

SERVES 4

4 slices good-quality white bread
½ cup peanut or canola oil
12 ounces fresh oyster mushrooms
6 plump garlic cloves, chopped
¼ cup fruity extra virgin olive oil
1½ teaspoons coarse sea salt
Freshly ground black pepper

Oyster mushrooms bridge the wild/domestic divide. They are native in much of North America and are also cultivated commercially. Quick grilling protects their delicate nature. Nothing tastes better than this simple appetizer of oyster mushrooms bathed in olive oil (one of our favorites is Spanish oil from Cazorla, in Andalusia, made from Royal olives) and garlic, then grilled and served on toast.

1. Toast the bread.

2. Heat the ½ cup of peanut oil in a skillet, and quickly sauté the toast in the hot oil. Transfer the toasts to individual plates and keep warm.

3. Preheat an indoor grill pan over medium-high heat.

4. While the pan is heating, separate the oyster mushrooms, keeping the pieces as large as possible, and brush off any dirt.

5. In a medium bowl, combine the mushrooms, garlic, olive oil, salt, and pepper to taste. Toss gently to coat the mushrooms with the other ingredients.

6. Place the mushrooms on the grill pan and grill, turning once or twice, until the edges start to brown and turn crisp and the garlic is very fragrant, 4 minutes. Immediately remove the mushrooms from the grill, place them on the toasts, and serve.

Wild Mushrooms en Papillote

SERVES 4

8 ounces fresh cremini
mushrooms

8 ounces fresh chanterelle or
black trumpet mushrooms,
or 4 ounces dried
chanterelles or black
trumpets rehydrated in
warm water for 20 minutes

8 ounces fresh oyster
mushrooms

4 ounces fresh enoki
mushrooms, optional

3 teaspoons dried thyme
leaves

1 teaspoon dried oregano

En papillote is a method of baking food that is wrapped in paper. It is most often used with fish: the fish and flavoring vegetables are baked inside a closed container made from the parchment. The most famous Creole dish prepared in this manner is pompano en papillote. The parchment prevents the juices and aromas of the baked ingredients from escaping. The technique of sealing ingredients in parchment paper works as well with mushrooms as it does with fish, and results in a delicious blending of flavors without the worry of overcooking.

1. Preheat the oven to 400° F.

2. In a medium bowl, toss the mushrooms, herbs, garlic, salt, and pepper with the olive oil.

3. Spread the mixture out onto a large baking dish or cookie

½ teaspoon minced fresh
  rosemary

1 teaspoon chopped fresh flat-
  leaf parsley

1 garlic clove, finely chopped

½ teaspoon salt

½ teaspoon freshly ground
  black pepper

¼ cup extra virgin olive oil

4 teaspoons unsalted
  butter

sheet, and roast in the oven for 5 minutes, or until the mush-rooms begin to wilt. Remove the dish from the oven.

4. Raise the oven temperature to 425° F. Cut out four 10-inch rounds of parchment paper.

5. Place a parchment circle in a wide, low-sided coffee cup. Fill the bottom with one-fourth of the roasted mushrooms. Top with 1 teaspoon of the butter. Bring together the top edges of the parchment, and tie with string forming a pouch. Place the pouch on a baking sheet. Repeat with the remaining parchment rounds. Place the baking sheet with the pouches in the oven and bake for 15 minutes, or until the paper browns. Cut and remove the string. Serve the mushrooms hot, in their parchment pouches.

Shiitake Mushrooms Rockefeller

24 to 32 fresh shiitake
   mushrooms of uniform size

¼ cup extra virgin olive oil

1 tablespoon salt

8 ounces fresh spinach

5 scallions

1½ cups chopped fennel fronds

2 cups (4 sticks) unsalted
   butter, at room temperature

1 cup fine dried bread crumbs

1 cup grated sharp Cheddar or
   Gruyère cheese

½ teaspoon Creole Seasoning
   Mix (page 37)

4 drops hot pepper sauce,
   such as Tabasco or Crystal

Shiitake Mushrooms

Shiitake mushrooms are superlative vegetarian "oysters." Select firm, plump mushrooms; they shouldn't be shriveled or dry in the least. Look for caps that curl down a bit at the edges—flat or concave caps indicate the mushrooms were too old when they were picked. The ideal shiitake also still has some white "fuzz" on the cap, but they're sometimes hard to find this way in supermarkets. Remember to save your shiitake stems for making stock—you can dry them until you have enough. Dry the stems in a 175° F oven for at least 1½ hours, or in a dryer used for drying fruit, until they're hard and brittle. Japanese and Chinese dried shiitakes have their own special uses and deep, earthy flavor, but for this dish, fresh mushrooms work best.

1. Preheat the oven to 350° F.

2. Remove the mushroom stems and reserve them for another use. Brush the caps clean, place them in a medium bowl, and toss with the olive oil.

3. Spread the mushrooms on a baking sheet and bake for 5 minutes, or until wilted. Remove, cover with plastic wrap, and refrigerate while you prepare the topping. (Mushrooms will keep 1 day in the refrigerator.)

4. Fill a medium saucepan with water and bring it to a boil. Add the salt, and then add the spinach, scallions, and fennel fronds. Cook for 1 minute. Then drain, reserving the blanching liquid, and rinse under cold water. Drain again, squeezing out any excess liquid.

5. Put the blanched vegetables into a blender, add about 2 tablespoons of the blanching liquid, and puree.

6. Transfer the puree to the bowl of a standing mixer, and using the dough hook or the mixing blade, combine it with the butter, bread crumbs, ½ cup of the cheese, the Creole Seasoning, and the hot pepper sauce. Cool the mixture in the refrigerator if necessary to create a moldable paste. (The filling can be made up to 1 day in advance but it is best, and most flavorful, if used immediately.)

7. When you are ready to serve the mushrooms, preheat the broiler.

8. Fill each mushroom with 1 to 2 teaspoons of the fennel mixture. Sprinkle the remaining ½ cup cheese over the mushrooms. Place them on a baking sheet and broil for 3 minutes, or until the mixture has softened and the cheese has thoroughly melted. Serve hot.

Medley of Garden Herbs and Blossoms with Mushrooms

SERVES 6

1 cup unbleached all-purpose flour

½ teaspoon salt

Peanut or sunflower oil

1 bottle (12 ounces) lager or pilsner beer

6 medium fresh oyster mushroom caps

6 fresh borage leaves

6 large fresh sage leaves

6 zucchini or other squash blossoms (check the insides for insects, but do not wash)

Though simple in preparation, this dish delights our guests. You can substitute a variety of other herb or vegetable leaves here, including arugula, flat-leaf parsley, or nasturtium leaves.

1. Mix the flour and salt in a bowl.

2. Pour oil to a depth of 2 inches in a heavy saucepan or deep-fat fryer, and place over medium heat.

3. Stir the beer into the flour, forming a bubbly batter that is just thick enough to thoroughly coat the mushrooms and herbs. Dip each mushroom, herb leaf, and blossom in the batter and let them drain on a wire rack for about 2 minutes.

4. Fry the mushroom caps first, until lightly browned. Remove them with a slotted spoon and drain them on paper towels. Then fry the herbs and zucchini blossoms, just until light golden brown, about 4 minutes. Arrange the medley on individual plates and serve hot.

Cornmeal-Crusted Oyster Mushrooms

1¼ cup yellow cornmeal

1 cup unbleached all-purpose
  flour

1 teaspoon cayenne pepper

¼ teaspoon freshly ground
  black or white pepper

1 teaspoon dried thyme or
  oregano

½ teaspoon onion or garlic
  powder

1 teaspoon salt

3 eggs

1 bottle (12 ounces) beer

Canola or safflower oil

1 pound large, firm oyster
  mushrooms

1. Combine the cornmeal, flour, cayenne pepper, black pepper, thyme, onion powder, and salt in a medium bowl. Mix thoroughly.

2. Beat the eggs in a bowl and stir in the beer.

3. Fill a large sauté pan with oil to a depth of 2 inches and heat over medium heat.

4. Coat the mushrooms by first dredging them in the flour mixture, then dipping them into the egg mixture, and again dipping them into the flour mixture. Place immediately in the hot oil. Fry the mushrooms, turning, until the corn crust is golden brown, 5 to 7 mintues.

Grilled Asparagus

20 fresh asparagus spears,
   tough ends trimmed

¼ cup extra virgin olive oil

1 teaspoon sea salt

1½ teaspoons freshly ground
   black pepper

1. On a plate, coat the asparagus spears in the olive oil. Sprinkle evenly with the salt and pepper. Set aside for 1 hour at room temperature.

2. Heat a grill pan over medium-high heat.

3. Place the asparagus on the grill, lower the heat to medium, and cook for about 10 minutes, turning frequently, until light brown grill marks appear. Remove the spears from the heat. Serve hot or cold.

Grilled Eggplant Tart

Pâte Brisée (recipe follows)

2 medium eggplants or 1 large
  eggplant

Extra virgin olive oil

1½ teaspoons sea salt

½ teaspoon freshly ground
  black pepper

6 garlic cloves, sliced

1 egg

3 tablespoons whole milk

1 tablespoon dried oregano, or
  3 tablespoons chopped
  fresh oregano

½ cup grated aged Canadian
  white Cheddar cheese

¾ cup coarsely chopped soft-
  bodied cheese, such as
  Camembert or Brie

SERVES 8 AS AN APPETIZER OR LIGHT ENTREE

One fine summer day we had planned to serve a classic onion tart for lunch, only to discover an hour before serving that we had run out of onions. We substituted grilled eggplant with oregano, and the results proved spectacular. It is critical here to use a good-quality soft cheese—Brie or Camembert.

1. Roll out the Pâte Brisée on a lightly floured surface to form a 12-inch round. Line a 9-inch tart pan with a removable bottom with the pastry, and place it in the freezer. Cover, and freeze 20 minutes, or up to 1 hour.

2. Preheat a large grill or sauté pan over medium heat.

3. Peel the eggplants, and cut them in half lengthwise. Cut the halves into ½-inch-wide slices, and then into fairly uniform strips of ⅓ inch. Place the strips in a bowl and lightly coat them with extra virgin olive oil. Sprinkle with the salt and pepper.

4. Grill or sauté the eggplant strips, turning once, until they char somewhat and become soft and *almost* fully cooked, 4 minutes on each side. Set them aside.

5. Preheat the oven to 375° F.

6. Heat 1 tablespoon extra virgin olive oil in a small pan over medium heat, and sauté the garlic for approximately 5 minutes, or until slightly caramelized. Set it aside.

7. Whisk the egg, the milk, and oregano together in a small mixing bowl.

8. Stir the garlic and eggplant strips together, and arrange them in the bottom of the tart pan. Pour the egg mixture over the eggplant and garlic, spreading the oregano evenly over the top of the tart. Top evenly with the cheeses.

9. Bake for about 40 minutes, or until the crust is golden and the cheese has browned. Remove the sides of the pan. Serve warm or cold.

Pâte Brisée

1 cup unbleached all-purpose
flour

7 tablespoons cold unsalted
butter, cut into thin slices

1 teaspoon salt

1 tablespoon confectioners'
sugar, optional

2 tablespoons cold whole milk

On a floured work surface or in a medium mixing bowl, blend together the flour, butter, salt, and optional sugar. Mash the flour and butter together with your hands, breaking the butter into small pieces. Add the milk and blend with the flour mixture, using quick hand motions. If the mixture doesn't hold together, add cold water, 1 tablespoon at time, until the dough forms a ball. Do not overwork the dough, or it will become tough. Form it into a ball, wrap it in plastic wrap, and refrigerate until ready to use, at which time the dough can be rolled out with a rolling pin on a floured work surface. The dough may be kept in a tightly sealed container for up to 1 week in the refrigerator.

Caramelized Fennel and Goat Cheese

SERVES 6

2 fennel bulbs (2 pounds
total), halved lengthwise,
cored, and sliced ¼ inch
thick (stems as well, if
available)

2 tablespoons extra virgin
olive oil

1 tablespoon coarse sea salt

2 teaspoons freshly ground
black pepper

3 ounces fresh goat cheese,
in large chunks

Fennel fronds, for garnish

The tartness of fresh chèvre and the anise taste of fennel are two essential flavors of the Mediterranean that appear in the cuisines of every country from the Levant to Spain. This dish evokes memories for many Trout Point guests who came from these areas.

1. Preheat the oven to 475° F.

2. On a large, rimmed baking sheet, toss the fennel with the olive oil. Season with the salt and pepper.

3. Roast in the oven, tossing the fennel every 10 minutes, until it is tender and caramelized around the edges, about 30 minutes.

4. Transfer the fennel to a bowl. Add the chunks of goat cheese and toss with the fennel until the cheese is slightly melted. Place on individual plates, garnish with fennel fronds, and serve.

Sweet Potato Cakes

2 cups finely grated sweet potatoes

2 tablespoons chopped onion

2 tablespoons chopped scallions (white and green parts)

Salt and freshly ground black pepper, to taste

¼ cup unbleached all-purpose flour

1 egg, beaten

2 tablespoons peanut or canola oil

6 whole chives (or 4, if serving as an entrée), for garnish

SERVES 6 AS AN APPETIZER OR 4 AS AN ENTRÉE

This sumptuous recipe uses a Creole Louisiana favorite—sweet potatoes—with the same ingenuity that is traditionally applied to crab cakes.

1. Combine the sweet potatoes, onion, scallions, salt and pepper, flour, and egg in a large bowl, and mix well. Hand-form into six patties (or four, if serving as an entrée).
2. Heat a large nonstick skillet over medium heat, and add the oil.
3. Fry the cakes in the hot oil until a browned crust has formed, 6 minutes on each side.
4. Garnish with the chives, and serve immediately.

Shrimp and Eggplant Risotto

16 medium shrimp

½ cup extra virgin olive oil

1 cup short-grain white rice, preferably Arborio

SERVES 6 AS AN APPETIZER OR 4 AS AN ENTRÉE

While shrimp may be the most flexible seafood, combining successfully with almost any vegetable, eggplant is not eager to dance with just any partner. Few foods combine as well as fresh shrimp and succulent eggplant.

1½ cups fragrant, dry white
  wine
2 cups Seafood Stock
  (page 65)
1 medium eggplant, unpeeled,
  cut into large pieces
3 tablespoons Asian fish sauce
  (see page 61)
2 tablespoons herbes de
  Provence
½ cup grated Parmigiano-
  Reggiano cheese
Sea salt

Risotto rice and genuine Parmesan cheese complete this dish. You can make an entree out of this risotto if you wish. It goes well with a light white wine, such as a Pinot Grigio from Italy or southern Ontario.

Perfect Risotto

The key to cooking risotto—once you have the freshest, most flavorful ingredients—is to cook the rice slowly, stirring over even heat, while adding enough liquid to prevent any burning. Always remember that any liquid you add will become part of the final flavor of the rice and sauce—wine, stock, and the natural juices of vegetables and seafood make for a savory combination. Keep the heat low and even, stir constantly but gently, add liquids as needed, and you will make perfect risotto!

1. Shell and devein the shrimp, placing the shells in a saucepan. Set the shrimp aside. Add ¾ cup water to the saucepan and bring to a boil. Simmer until the liquid is reduced to ½ cup, about 20 minutes. Strain the shells, reserving the liquid. Discard the shells and set the liquid aside.

2. Heat the olive oil in a deep, heavy skillet or a Dutch oven over medium heat until it is fragrant but not smoking. (Do not overheat.)

3. Add the rice and cook, stirring constantly, for about 3 minutes, or until it begins to change color. Add the wine, a little at a time, cooking until it is almost absorbed. When the rice has absorbed all the wine, begin adding the reserved shrimp water, little by little, stirring constantly and adjusting the heat to maintain a low simmer. Then begin to add small amounts of the Seafood Stock, stirring until each addition is absorbed before adding more.

4. When the rice is beginning to soften, about 20 minutes cooking time, add the eggplant pieces. Keep cooking and stirring and adding stock.

5. When the eggplant is starting to soften, 8 to 10 minutes, add the fish sauce, herbes de Provence, and shrimp. Keep adding stock and stirring until the rice is al dente, 35 to 40 min-

utes total cooking time. You don't have to use all the stock—let the texture of the rice guide you. The mixture should be a little soupy.

6. Stir in the cheese, mix well, and season with salt to taste. Serve hot.

Saffron Lobster Risotto

SERVES 4

3 tablespoons extra virgin
  olive oil
1 cup short-grain white rice,
  preferably Arborio
1 cup dry white wine
5 cups Seafood Stock (page
  65), preferably made with
  shrimp or lobster shells
¼ cup sultana (golden) raisins,
  soaked in ⅓ cup white
  rum for 30 minutes at
  room temperature and
  strained
1 generous pinch saffron
  threads
1½ tablespoons Asian fish
  sauce (see page 61)
1½ cups coarsely chopped
  steamed lobster meat
¼ cup grated Parmigiano-
  Reggiano cheese
Sea salt

Guests exclaim over this rich risotto, in which we use fresh, succulent Yarmouth County lobster combined with the exquisite flavor of the saffron we bring back each year from Spain. The sultana raisins accentuate the sweetness of the lobster meat.

1. Heat the olive oil in a deep, heavy skillet or a Dutch oven over medium heat until it is fragrant but not smoking. (Do not overheat.)

2. Add the rice and cook, stirring constantly, for about 3 minutes, or until it begins to change color. Add the wine, a little at a time, cooking until it is almost absorbed. Then begin adding the Seafood Stock, little by little, stirring. Adjust the heat as needed to maintain a low simmer, and let each addition of stock be absorbed before adding the next.

3. When the rice is beginning to soften, about 20 minutes cooking time, add the sultanas and half the saffron. Keep cooking and stirring and gradually adding stock.

4. When the rice is like a firm porridge, add the fish sauce, the remaining saffron, and the lobster. Keep adding stock and cooking and stirring until the rice is al dente, 35 to 40 minutes total cooking time. You don't have to use all the

stock—let the texture of the rice guide you. The mixture should be a little soupy.

5. Stir in the cheese, mix well, and season with salt to taste. Serve hot.

Wine-Braised Artichokes with Shrimp

16 small to medium artichokes
with stems 1 to 2 inches in
length

¼ cup extra virgin olive oil

½ cup dry white wine

1 tablespoon herbes de
Provence

½ teaspoon salt

6 ounces aged, firm goat
cheese or Parmigiano-
Reggiano, coarsely chopped

1 pound medium shrimp,
shelled and deveined

The technique of first frying artichokes and then steaming them in wine makes for a faultless preparation that reminds us of summer days in New Orleans. Though many people associate artichokes with Mediterranean cuisine, they grow well in the warm climate of New Orleans and have been a staple of cuisine in the Crescent City for decades, if not centuries.

In choosing artichokes, look for tender green leaves that fade to a cream color at the base, without blemishes or brown spots. You do not have to remove the "choke" when the artichokes are young and small. If you can find only large artichokes, then cut them in half, remove the choke, and proceed with the recipe.

1. Trim the stems of the artichokes evenly. Remove the tough outer leaves. Turning the artichoke three or four times, trim off the top third of the remaining leaves at an angle with a sharp knife.

2. Place a deep skillet over medium heat and add the olive oil. Heat until the oil is hot but not smoking.

3. Add the artichokes, turning or flipping them in the pan to coat them with the oil. Fry the artichokes for 5 minutes, or until the outer leaves just start to crisp.

4. Add ¼ cup of the wine and sauté for about 5 minutes.

5. Add the remaining ¼ cup wine, the herbes de Provence, and the salt. Cover, and reduce

the heat to a simmer. Cook for 10 minutes, or until the artichoke stems are soft.

6. Uncover, and if there is excess liquid, simmer until it is reduced. Then add the cheese, allowing it to melt partially.

7. Mix in the shrimp, and cook until they turn pink, 3 to 5 minutes. Serve immediately.

Mediterranean-Style Artichokes

SERVES 4

8 medium, very fresh
 artichokes
¼ cup olive oil
¼ cup peanut or canola oil
Sea salt

1. Peel off the tough outer leaves (3 to 5 layers) of the artichokes. Trim and peel the stems. Using a large chef's knife, cut off the top one-fourth to one-third of each artichoke. Slice the artichokes in half lengthwise.

2. Place a deep skillet over medium heat and add the oils. Heat until the oils are hot but not smoking. Fry the artichokes until golden and crisp on each side, about 10 minutes. (Some charring is okay.) When they are almost done (the outer leaves pull away easily and the heart is tender when pierced with a fork), add about ½ cup water to the pan, cover, and steam for 3 minutes. Uncover, and finish frying for up to 2 minutes, until any excess liquid has evaporated. Sprinkle with salt. Serve hot.

Tuna Tartare

SERVES 6

4 ounces very-high-quality
 fresh tuna
1 tablespoon capers, coarsely
 chopped
2 tablespoons fresh lemon
 juice

Following the Gulf Stream north, fresh tuna comes into Yarmouth, Nova Scotia, every day from the end of June until the end of August, and sometimes later. To judge fresh tuna's quality, look for firm flesh that is still bright red and juicy, not grayish, dull, or dry. The flesh will have visible distinct bands, usually from ¼ to ½ inch thick.

½ teaspoon salt

¼ teaspoon freshly ground black pepper

1 teaspoon finely chopped hot chile, such as Serrano or habañero

1½ tablespoons extra virgin olive oil

1 tablespoon heavy cream

1 cucumber, cut into thin slices

The bands in the meat should hold together and not separate while raw. Of course, tuna should never smell fishy or strong, and if there's still skin on the meat, it should appear shiny, with deep blue-gray colors. Without these qualities, the fish may not be at its best. The freshness of the fish is especially important for making tartare.

1. Using a chef's knife, cut the tuna into small cubes, and then chop it as finely as possible.

2. Combine the capers, lemon juice, salt, pepper, and chile in a medium bowl. Add the tuna and mix thoroughly. Place the mixture in the refrigerator for 10 minutes. Then mix in the olive oil and cream, and refrigerate for another 5 minutes.

3. Use a small cup to form individual portions of the tartare, and place each portion in the center of a plate. Arrange the cucumber slices around the tartare, and serve.

Trout Point Gravlax

SERVES 12

1 orange or lemon

3 tablespoons salt

2 tablespoons sugar

2 tablespoons olive oil

2 tablespoons white rum, plain vodka, or grappa

½ teaspoon cracked black pepper

½ teaspoon crushed fennel seeds

2 pounds thick salmon steaks, skin on

The inspiration for our gravlax came from a family restaurant in Rieti, Italy, where the chef kindly wrote out instructions for the salmon we so admired one night. We perfected the recipe through several summers at Trout Point, using our superlative fresh Nova Scotia salmon. Be sure to use only the freshest salmon, ideally steaks 1½ inches to 2 inches thick. Serve the gravlax with Crème Fraîche (page 47) and toasted Tusket Brown Whole-Grain Bread (page 169).

1. Squeeze the juice from the orange into a deep glass or ce-

ramic dish, discarding the pulp. Thinly slice the orange peel; add it to the juice. Stir in the salt, sugar, olive oil, rum, pepper, and fennel, combining thoroughly.

2. Place the salmon steaks in the dish, cover, and refrigerate.

3. Marinate for 3 days, turning the fish over at least twice a day.

4. Serve thinly sliced.

Smoked Trout Cakes

½ cup finely chopped white
   onion
½ cup chopped green bell
   pepper
¼ cup chopped celery
10 ounces smoked trout or
   smoked salmon, coarsely
   chopped
1 cup dried bread crumbs
½ teaspoon cayenne pepper
½ teaspoon freshly ground
   black pepper
½ teaspoon dried thyme leaves
¼ teaspoon garlic powder
¼ cup grated aged Cheddar
   cheese
½ teaspoon salt
1 egg, lightly beaten
¼ cup olive or peanut oil
Salmon Cake Sauce (page 120)
   or your favorite
   tartar sauce

SERVES 4

We smoke our own seafood (see Chapter 8) for recipes like this one, but you can use store-bought trout or salmon if you haven't had time to set up your backyard smokehouse yet.

1. In a medium mixing bowl, combine the onion, bell pepper, celery, trout, and ¾ cup of the bread crumbs. Toss lightly. Add the cayenne, black pepper, thyme, garlic powder, Cheddar, and salt. Toss to combine thoroughly. Then add the egg, and combine until the mixture is thick enough to form patties. Make eight small patties.

2. Spread the remaining ¼ cup bread crumbs on a plate, and coat the patties in the crumbs.

3. Heat a large nonstick skillet over medium heat. Add the oil, and tilt the pan to coat the surface. Add the patties and sauté until golden brown, about 4 minutes per side. Serve hot, topped with the Salmon Cake Sauce.

Scallop and Haddock Terrine with Pistachios

½ cup whole salted pistachios

1 pound fresh scallops

1 pound fresh haddock fillets,
  cut into pieces

1½ pounds Salmon Bacon
  (page 212) or smoked
  salmon

8 tablespoons (1 stick) butter,
  at room temperature

¼ cup Madeira

1 egg, beaten

¾ cup chopped white onions
  or shallots

1½ tablespoons unbleached
  all-purpose flour

1½ tablespoons herbes de
  Provence

1½ tablespoons sea salt

1½ tablespoons cracked black
  pepper

We use homemade salmon bacon to line this terrine. You can substitute regular smoked salmon, but try to get pieces with as much fat in them as possible. The blending of scallops and fresh haddock makes for a subtle seafood flavor, which is rounded out with the crunchy pistachios. If you do not have any Madeira on hand, substitute a cream sherry or Pedro Ximénez.

Toasting Nuts and Seeds

Heat a thick, cast iron or other heavy-bottomed skillet over low heat. Place the nuts in the pan in a single layer so that every individual nut has contact with the pan. Toast, stirring every 4 to 5 minutes, for a total of about 20 minutes. The nuts should brown slightly and have a pleasant aroma, but never burn. Slow heating is the goal so that the entire nut, not just the exterior, is toasted. This can be used for almonds, chestnuts, walnuts, sesame seeds, peanuts, etc.

1. Preheat the oven to 340° F.

2. Heat a small skillet over medium heat, add the pistachios, and toast, stirring, until fragrant and lightly browned, about 5 minutes. Set them aside.

3. Combine the scallops, haddock, 4 ounces of the Salmon Bacon, and 7 tablespoons of the butter in a food processor, and puree.

4. Transfer the puree to a medium bowl and add the pistachios, Madeira, egg, onion, flour, herbes de Provence, salt, and pepper. Mix thoroughly.

5. Grease a standard loaf pan or terrine with the remaining 1 tablespoon butter. Line the terrine with the remaining Salmon Bacon, arranging the slices so they extend from the top

of one side, across the bottom, and up the other side. Finish by lining the two ends. (You should have enough slices left to cover the top.)

6. Using a rubber spatula, fill the lined terrine with the scallop mixture. Smooth the top, and arrange the remaining Salmon Bacon slices over the mixture.

7. Place the terrine in a larger baking dish and add water to reach three-quarters of the way up the sides of the terrine. Bake for 1¼ hours, or until the terrine begins to pull away from the sides of the pan and liquid fat is visible in the gaps. Remove the pan from the water bath and allow it to cool for at least 1 hour. Then unmold the terrine onto a serving plate. Place it in the refrigerator for at least 4 hours. Serve in slices. (The terrine can be refrigerated for up to 1 week.)

Swordfish Terrine with Smoked Sea Trout

For the panada

1 cup whole milk

2 tablespoons unsalted butter

½ teaspoon sea salt

½ teaspoon freshly ground
black pepper

¼ teaspoon ground nutmeg

1 cup unbleached all-purpose
flour

2 eggs

For the terrine

5 tablespoons unsalted butter

1 shallot, finely chopped

1½ pounds swordfish fillets,
skin removed

1 tablespoon sea salt

½ tablespoon white pepper

⅛ teaspoon ground nutmeg

1 teaspoon dried thyme leaves

⅛ teaspoon dry mustard

¾ cup heavy cream

1 egg white, lightly beaten

4 ounces thinly sliced smoked
sea trout or other smoked
fish

This terrine is prepared in two easy steps: first, making the *panada*, which acts as a binder, and then adding the panada to the swordfish in the food processor.

Prepare the panada

1. Combine the milk, butter, salt, pepper, and nutmeg in a small saucepan and bring to a boil over medium heat. Add the flour, beating vigorously and continuously until it has been thoroughly mixed in. Once the mixture forms a distinct ball and easily pulls away from the sides of the pan, 3 to 6 minutes, transfer it to a bowl to cool slightly. When the flour mixture is warm instead of hot, add 1 egg and mix it in thoroughly. Add the second egg and repeat. Cover, and set the panada aside in a cool place. (May be prepared up to 1 day in advance.)

Prepare the terrine

2. Preheat the oven to 340°. Grease a standard loaf pan or terrine with butter. Fill a large bowl with ice.

3. Melt 1 tablespoon of the butter in a medium skillet over medium heat, and sauté the shallot until wilted, about 3 minutes. Set aside.

4. Cut the swordfish into thin strips. Combine the salt, pepper, nutmeg, thyme, and mustard in a bowl. Add the swordfish strips, and toss to coat. Place the coated swordfish and shallot in a food processor and process thoroughly, ensuring that the entire mixture has become completely minced. Add the panada and process again until thoroughly mixed. Transfer the mixture to a stainless steel bowl and set it in the larger bowl of ice.

5. Whip the heavy cream until soft peaks form. Fold in the egg white and then the whipped cream into the swordfish mixture.

6. Fill the prepared terrine pan halfway with swordfish mixture, and top with the slices of smoked sea trout. Spread the remaining swordfish mixture on top. Cover with the remaining 4 tablespoons butter, thinly sliced.

7. Place the terrine in a larger baking dish, and add water to reach three-quarters of the way up the sides of the terrine. Bake for 45 minutes, or until the terrine begins to pull away from the sides of the pan and liquid fat is visible in the gaps. Remove the terrine from the water bath and allow it to cool for at least 1 hour. Then unmold the terrine onto a serving plate. Cover, and refrigerate the terrine for at least 4 hours before serving. Serve in slices. (The terrine can be kept in the refrigerator for up to 1 week.)

Mussels in White Wine and Garlic

¼ cup extra virgin olive oil

10 garlic cloves, coarsely chopped

1 small onion, cut in half and sliced

1 tablespoon dried thyme leaves

¼ green or red bell pepper, sliced

1 teaspoon coarsely ground black pepper

2 bay leaves

¾ cup dry white wine

3 pounds fresh mussels, cleaned and debearded

Marc Lescarbot reported in 1609 that *moules* were a mainstay enjoyed equally on the coasts of Brittany and Nova Scotia, even in winter. To this day mussels are among the finest of our local shellfish. Spaniards, Italians, and Turks love them too, as we've found in our travels. These mussels will warm you up on cold fall or winter days, and are best enjoyed accompanied with a hearty bread, like the Herb Garden Bread (page 175), alongside to sop up the delicious sauce. You can prepare the sauce (through Step 3) a couple of hours in advance, and then cook the mussels when you are ready to serve them. We find that a paella pan with a lid works well for this dish. Be sure to cook the onions and garlic slowly— you do not want any hint of burnt flavor.

Mussels

Mussels, like most shellfish, should be stored in the refrigerator in a container that allows them to breathe, and they should be kept moist. When stored properly, they can be kept up to three days. Markets often put mussels in sealed plastic bags for purchase, cutting off their vital air supply and making it impossible to keep them for more than a day or two. Before cooking, soak mussels briefly in a pot of water, debeard them, and then rinse them in a colander, picking out any individuals that have cracked shells or that are obviously dead, or on the doorstep.

1. Place a pot that is large enough to hold all the mussels once they open over medium-low heat, and add the olive oil. Slowly cook the garlic and onion in the oil until their internal

sugars are released and they turn soft and begin to brown, 7 to 10 minutes. Be careful not to burn the garlic.

2. Add the thyme, bell pepper, black pepper, and bay leaves. Cook for 2 minutes.

3. Turn the heat to high, add the wine, and cook until only a thin layer of liquid remains, 30 to 60 seconds.

4. Add the mussels, stir them into the sauce, and cover. Cook just until the mussels open, 4 to 6 minutes. (Discard any that do not open.) Stir the mussels once more to coat them evenly with the sauce. Serve in a large bowl or directly from the pan.

Wild Mussels with Tomatoes and Red Peppers

1 large ripe tomato, coarsely chopped

½ red bell pepper, sliced

3 tablespoons dried red chiles, hot or sweet, chopped

¼ cup extra virgin olive oil

5 garlic cloves, crushed with the side of a knife

3 tablespoons light red wine

2 pounds fresh mussels, cleaned and debearded

SERVES 4

This is an easy and colorful way to serve mussels, one of the favorite shellfish enjoyed at Port Royal, Nova Scotia, by the Ordre de Bon Temps in 1607. You shouldn't need to add any salt, as these delectable creatures bring their own to the table.

1. Mix the tomato, bell pepper, and dried chiles in a medium bowl, and set aside.

2. Over medium heat, heat the olive oil in a pot that is large enough to hold the mussels. Sauté the garlic for about 5 minutes, until the pieces start to crisp and brown.

3. Add the tomato/pepper mixture and the wine, and cook over high heat. Cook until the liquid is reduced slightly and the tomato is softened, about 7 minutes. Do not overcook. (The mixture can be prepared up to 4 hours ahead; keep it covered and at room temperature. When you are ready to cook the mussels, heat the pan over high heat until the mixture starts to simmer.)

4. Add the mussels, toss once or twice to coat them with the sauce, then cover the pot. Cook just until most of the mussels have opened, 4 to 6 minutes. Do not overcook them, or they will lose their tenderness and flavor. Discard any that have not opened. Toss again in the sauce, and serve immediately.

Shrimp and Green Olive Tart

SERVES 8 AS AN APPETIZER OR LIGHT ENTRÉE

2 tablespoons extra virgin
   olive oil
6 ounces medium shrimp
   (about 1 cup), shelled and
   deveined
Freshly ground black pepper
Pâte Brisée (page 14)
1½ cups fine imported green
   olives, pitted
2 large eggs, whisked until
   frothy
2 teaspoons fresh thyme
   leaves, or 1 teaspoon fragrant
   dried thyme leaves
¾ cup grated Manchego or
   Gruyère cheese, or ¾ cup
   crumbled fresh goat cheese

The fresh flavors of green olives and savory shrimp complement one another perfectly in this tart. Find the best, most flavorful green olives; they should be young, firm, and barely cured, if possible. Use brine-cured, not oil-cured, olives for this recipe.

1. Preheat the oven to 400° F.
2. Heat the olive oil in a medium skillet over medium heat just until it becomes fragrant. Add the shrimp, season with pepper, and sauté for about 2 minutes. They shouldn't be fully cooked. Remove the skillet from the heat.
3. Roll out the Pâte Brisée on a lightly floured surface to form a 12-inch round. Place the dough in a greased or non-stick tart pan with a removable bottom, and bake until it just starts to turn golden, about 10 minutes.
4. Arrange the shrimp and the olives in the bottom of the tart shell. Pour in the eggs, sprinkle with the thyme, and top with the cheese.

5. Bake just until the egg sets and the cheese is melted and golden, about 20 minutes. Cool for 10 minutes on a wire rack. Remove the sides of the pan. Serve warm or cold.

Shrimp and Scallop Ceviche

1 pound mixed fresh scallops and shrimp, shelled and deveined

1½ cups fresh lime or lemon juice

1 tomato, chopped

1 small onion, very finely chopped

4 Serrano chiles, finely chopped

¼ cup extra virgin olive oil

½ teaspoon dried oregano or thyme leaves

2 tablespoons chopped fresh cilantro

Salt and freshly ground black pepper

Along with Trout Point Gravlax (page 21) and Tuna Tartare (page 20), ceviche could belong in anthropologist Claude Lévi-Strauss's *The Raw and the Cooked*, a famous book that explores the cultural importance of uncooked versus cooked foods. Ceviche, like gravlax, integrates the two by "cooking" over time with citrus juices, using the Old World oranges, limes, and lemons to create a purely New World and Creole dish. No appetizer more clearly characterizes Latin Creole cuisine than ceviche. If you use absolutely fresh seafood and add citrus and chile flavors, you'll be astounded by how satisfying this combination can be. We often serve ceviche in chilled martini glasses with delicate slices of toasted Herb Garden Bread (page 175).

1. Place the scallops and shrimp in a nonreactive metal, ceramic, or glass bowl or dish. (A nonreactive container is important because of the acidity in this recipe.)

2. Pour the lime juice over the seafood, fully coating it. Cover, and chill for up to 6 hours, turning several times to ensure that everything marinates and that the citric acid has time to "cook" everything thoroughly.

3. Combine the tomato, onion, chiles, olive oil, oregano, and cilantro in a medium bowl. Add salt and pepper to taste. Pour in the juice from the seafood mixture, and mix well.

4. Add the seafood, mix well, and allow the mixture to marinate for at least 1 hour. Serve.

Scallops en Brochette

8 ounces smoked swordfish, smoked salmon, or other smoked fish, very thinly sliced

2 tablespoons unbleached all-purpose flour

¼ teaspoon salt

¼ teaspoon freshly ground black pepper

2 egg whites, lightly beaten

1 pound fresh scallops

1 cup peanut oil

Chopped fresh chives

Applying New Orleans know-how to local Nova Scotia seafood, we came up with this new *en brochette* recipe, using fresh, sweet scallops in place of the usual oysters, and our own smoked swordfish instead of bacon. Simple as it is, the meaty, smoky flavors of the fish penetrate the succulent scallops and make for a real treat. You will want to soak wooden skewers in water for about an hour before you use them, so that they won't burn.

1. Cut the swordfish into ½-inch-thick strips. Blend the flour, salt, and pepper together in a small bowl. Place the egg whites in a shallow bowl.

2. Wrap each scallop with a swordfish strip. (Use toothpicks if they won't stay in place). Dip each scallop into the egg whites, lightly coating it, and then dust with the flour mixture.

3. Using short wooden or metal skewers, skewer the wrapped scallops through the center, 4 or 5 scallops per skewer. Place the skewers on a baking sheet.

4. Heat the oil in a deep, heavy frying pan or a Dutch oven. When the oil is hot, fry the brochettes for 3 minutes. Turn, and fry for an additional 3 minutes. Serve immediately, garnished with the chopped chives.

Quahogs Florentine on the Half-Shell

7 quahogs, or about 14 smaller
  clams

3 tablespoons unsalted butter

6 ounces fresh spinach, finely
  chopped

2½ tablespoons finely
  chopped celery

2½ tablespoons finely
  chopped scallions (white
  parts only)

2½ tablespoons finely
  chopped fennel

3 tablespoons finely chopped
  fresh flat-leaf parsley

½ teaspoon freshly ground
  black pepper

¼ teaspoon cayenne pepper

Salt

3 tablespoons Herbsaint
  liqueur

2 tablespoons dried bread
  crumbs

¾ cup shredded aged
  Canadian white Cheddar

This adaptation of the classic New Orleans Oysters Rockefeller provides an excellent way to use quahogs—the largest of clams—and makes for a beautiful presentation. If you can't find Herbsaint, a liqueur still made in New Orleans, you can substitute Pernod or another anise-flavored liqueur.

1. Fill a large saucepan with water to a depth of ¾ inch. Bring to a boil over high heat. Add the quahogs and cover. Boil until the quahog shells just open, 3 to 8 minutes, taking out the quahogs as soon as they open, and leaving the others to continue cooking. Do not overcook them or the meat will become tough. Remove the meat from the shells and mince, reserving the shells. (The leftover boiling liquid can be strained and used as a seafood stock, such as for Finnan Haddie Jambalaya on page 152.)

2. Melt the butter in a large skillet over medium heat, add the spinach, celery, scallions, fennel, and parsley, and sauté until soft, about 7 minutes.

3. Add the black pepper, cayenne, and salt to taste. Then add the minced clams, mixing thoroughly. Add the Herbsaint and immediately remove the pan from the heat. Stir in the bread crumbs.

4. Preheat the broiler.

5. Fill the quahog shells evenly with the clam-vegetable mixture, and top each one with a thin layer of cheese.

6. Place the filled shells on a baking sheet and broil until the cheese has melted and is beginning to brown, about 2 minutes. Remove from the oven and serve.

Oysters Rockefeller

1 pound fresh spinach, coarsely chopped, or one 10-ounce package frozen spinach

¼ cup fresh flat-leaf parsley leaves

¼ cup chopped scallions (white and green parts) or shallots

1 cup bread crumbs

1 cup grated Gruyère or sharp Cheddar cheese

1 tablespoon Creole Seasoning Mix (recipes follow), or to taste

1 tablespoon Worcestershire sauce

1½ cups (3 sticks) unsalted butter, at room temperature

3 tablespoons Pernod

12 fresh oysters in the shell

Oysters and spinach have a natural affinity. A dash of Pernod, or of any of the drier anise-flavored liqueurs such as the Herbsaint of New Orleans, rounds out the flavor. Oysters Rockefeller is a famous dish, and New Orleans restaurateurs cautiously guard their recipes. But in fact, the combination of spinach with shellfish long predates the colonial history of New Orleans. Traditionally, the oysters are baked on an open half-shell or in an ovenproof dish that resembles six oyster half-shells.

1. Preheat the oven to 450° F. Fill a large bowl with ice water.

2. Bring a saucepan of water to a boil. Add the spinach, parsley, and scallions, and cook for 1 minute. Immediately drain the blanched vegetables in a colander, reserving 2 tablespoons of the cooking water, and then plunge the colander into the bowl of ice water. When the vegetables are cool, drain thoroughly. Squeeze out the excess liquid.

3. Place the greens in a food processor, add the reserved 2 tablespoons cooking water, and puree.

4. In a mixing bowl, blend together the bread crumbs, cheese, Creole Seasoning Mix, Worcestershire, butter, and Pernod. Stir until well mixed.

5. Thoroughly combine the spinach mixture with the butter mixture.

6. Place each oyster in a half-shell on a baking sheet. Mound the spinach mixture over each oyster. Bake until slightly golden and heated through, 6 to 10 minutes.

Serve immediately.

Creole Seasoning Mix 1

1 tablespoon salt

1 teaspoon white pepper

1 teaspoon freshly ground
  black pepper

¼ teaspoon cayenne pepper

½ teaspoon dried thyme leaves

½ teaspoon garlic powder

½ teaspoon onion powder

MAKES ABOUT 2 TABLESPOONS

Stir all the ingredients together in a small bowl. Stored in an airtight jar, this will keep for up to 2 months.

Creole Seasoning Mix 2

2 teaspoons salt

1 teaspoon onion powder

1 teaspoon garlic powder

½ teaspoon white pepper

½ teaspoon freshly ground
  black pepper

½ teaspoon cayenne pepper

¼ teaspoon dried thyme leaves

¼ teaspoon dried basil

Optional

¼ teaspoon filé powder
  (see page 152)

¼ teaspoon dried oregano

¼ teaspoon crumbled dried
  rosemary

¼ teaspoon dry mustard

MAKES ABOUT 2 TABLESPOONS

Stir all the ingredients together in a small bowl. Stored in an airtight jar, this will keep for up to 2 months.

Chapter two

Soups

But many times the Savages living near us have caught some quantity of Sturgeon, Salmon, or meals of fish. . . . With regard to fish, there are Porpoise and Puffers in such abundance that the sea appears covered over. But if one lacks the things necessary to fish, then one can rely solely on the shellfish, like Oysters, Clams, Ciguenaux, and others, with which one can content oneself.

—Marc Lescarbot, *Histoire de la Nouvelle-France,* 1609

Gathering ingredients for cooking reconnects us with the land and sea, and soups brimming with wild-harvested foods truly bring us back to the primordial. At Trout Point, fresh soup begins each lunch and dinner. Soups allow for creativity, particularly when one has a great stock or broth to work with. As part of a four- to six-course meal, the soups at Trout Point are rich and robust but do not overwhelm the appetite. We often use seafood as a seasoning ingredient to complement our freshly picked vegetables or wild mushrooms. Many of Trout Point's soups reflect the bounty of the Atlantic, giving a true sense of place in their richness and complex flavors.

Soups warm the senses and entice them for what will follow. Our soups are welcoming, colorful, and surprising, and put everyone in a good mood for the rest of the meal.

Soup Basics

A good stock forms the basis for all great soups. Some soups require some advance planning, but with a prepared homemade stock or even a good commercial product, you can often construct a soup within ten or twenty minutes.

Good kitchen equipment is essential. A soup pot or stockpot should have a heavy bottom. Ideally the pot should be cast iron, or stainless steel with a substantial cladding of aluminum or copper (with the aluminum or copper extending well up the sides, not just covering the bottom, to provide for pure, even heating). We use American All-Clad and French Bourgeat pots in the Lodge kitchen. Heavy-duty copper-exterior pots also radiate and retain heat well, but they are more expensive.

Cauliflower-Leek Soup with Brie

SERVES 4

2 leeks (white parts only), trimmed and well rinsed

¼ cup plus 2 tablespoons extra virgin olive oil

1 onion, chopped

1 green bell pepper, chopped

1 head cauliflower, broken into florets

4 cups Vegetable Stock (page 55)

½ teaspoon chopped fresh rosemary

½ teaspoon chopped fresh thyme

½ teaspoon chopped fresh marjoram

Cauliflower provides a marvelous base for the savory leeks and rich Brie in this soup. Fresh herbs add a finishing touch of flavor.

1. Preheat a grill pan over high heat. Pat the leeks dry and coat with 2 tablespoons of the olive oil. Grill the leeks, turning frequently, until slightly charred, about 8 minutes. Chop the leeks.

2. Heat the remaining oil in a large saucepan over medium heat. Add the onion and bell pepper, and cook until the onion is transparent, 7 to 8 minutes.

3. Add the cauliflower and the leeks, cover, and cook over low heat until the cauliflower is almost soft, about 15 minutes. Add the stock and bring to a boil. Reduce the heat to a simmer, and cook until the cauliflower is soft, 5 to 6 more minutes.

¼ teaspoon dried lavender
  flowers
½ teaspoon chopped fresh
  sage
8 ounces Brie cheese

4. Transfer two-thirds of the mixture to a blender or food processor, and puree. Return the puree to the saucepan, add the herbs, and simmer for 15 minutes.

5. Add the Brie to the soup and stir until it has melted. Serve immediately.

Chilled Cream of Sweet Potato

SERVES 4

1 large sweet potato

2 tablespoons olive oil

¼ ounce smoked salmon, cut
  into pieces

4 tablespoons (½ stick)
  unsalted butter

1 small onion, minced

½ green bell pepper, minced

1 shallot, chopped

¼ cup unbleached all-purpose
  flour

5 cups Seafood Stock (page 65)
  or Vegetable Stock (page 55)

1 bay leaf

1 teaspoon minced jalapeño
  pepper

½ cup heavy cream

This rich soup is not for those counting fat grams. It can be a meal itself or, in small portions, a super summer appetizer. While the sweet potato speaks of Louisiana, the addition of pan-fried smoked salmon brings in the flavors of Acadie. At Trout Point, we smoke our own salmon and often use it as a substitute for bacon or other smoked meats. Pan-frying extracts the salmon's distinct flavor and enhances its texture.

1. Preheat the oven to 350° F. Scrub the sweet potato. Place it on a foil-lined baking sheet and roast it until it is tender and a fork can be inserted easily, about 55 minutes.

2. While the potato is roasting, heat the oil in a small skillet and fry the salmon until slightly crisp, about 3 minutes. Set it aside.

3. Melt the butter in a stockpot or large saucepan over medium heat. Add the onion, bell pepper, and shallot, and cook until the onion is caramelized, about 10 minutes.

4. Sprinkle the flour over the vegetables and stir it into the mixture. Add the sweet potatoes and stir well. Cook for 2 minutes.

5. Pour the stock into the pot, stirring constantly. Add the bay leaf and bring to a boil. Reduce the heat and simmer for 5 minutes. Then stir in the jalapeño and the cream and remove the pot from the heat. Cover, and chill for at least 1 hour. Remove the bay leaf before serving.

Warm Sweet Potato Soup

SERVES 4

1 large sweet potato

¼ cup plus 2 tablespoons peanut or canola oil

1 onion, chopped

¼ cup chopped green bell pepper

4 cups Vegetable Stock (page 55)

Salt and freshly ground black pepper

2 tablespoons chopped fresh chervil

Sweet potatoes are a Louisiana staple. The best come from around Opelousas, which also gave us Louisiana's best-known contemporary chef, Paul Prudhomme.

1. Peel the sweet potato, and grate it on a box grater or in a food processor.

2. Heat the oil in a skillet over medium heat. Add the onion, bell pepper, and sweet potato, reduce the heat to low, cover, and cook until the sweet potato is caramelized, about 12 minutes.

3. Stir the mixture and allow the surface of the sweet potato to caramelize a second time, about 5 minutes.

4. Pour the Vegetable Stock into a saucepan or stockpot, and bring to a simmer over medium heat. Add the sweet potato mixture and cook for 10 minutes. Remove the pot from the heat, and allow to cool slightly.

5. Transfer the mixture to a blender, and puree.

6. Return the pureed soup to the saucepan, and reheat it. Season with salt and pepper. Just before serving, stir in the chervil.

Rosemary-Scented Potato and Onion Soup

SERVES 4

1 tablespoon peanut oil

1 onion, grated

2 ounces smoked fish, such as
   haddock or pollock, flaked

2 medium potatoes, grated

4 cups Vegetable Stock
   (page 55)

½ red bell pepper, diced

½ teaspoon dried rosemary

2 tablespoons shrimp paste

1 tablespoon unsalted butter

Herbs grow extremely well in the soil of Nova Scotia, and rosemary especially thrives here, forming big, woody plants in the Lodge's organic garden. Potatoes are an Acadian staple, as they have been for poor areas around the Western world (in Louisiana, it was the sweet potato). Acadians and Cajuns smoked fish and meat to preserve them and to increase their inherent flavors. The flavors of carefully smoked foods are critical to the delicious, deep flavors of New World Creole cuisine. Smoked haddock is a good choice for this soup, though you can use any smoked fish or shellfish.

1. Heat the peanut oil in a saucepan or stockpot over medium heat. Add the onion and cook until lightly caramelized, about 8 minutes (do not overcook).

2. Add the smoked fish and sauté for 1 minute.

3. Add the potatoes, Vegetable Stock, bell pepper, rosemary, shrimp paste, and butter. Bring to a simmer. Reduce the heat to low, and cook for about 10 minutes. Serve hot.

Beet and Truffle Soup

2 pounds beets, stems
trimmed to 1 inch

1 cup Mushroom Stock (recipe
follows), made with porcini
mushrooms

4 cups Chicken Stock (page
60) or Vegetable Stock
(page 55)

2 tablespoons extra virgin
olive oil

3 garlic cloves, smashed with
the side of a knife

3 dried red chiles, such as
pepperoncino, chopped

½ cup chopped onion

½ cup chopped green bell
pepper

1 tablespoon caraway seeds,
crushed

1 tablespoon freshly ground
black pepper

1 tablespoon unbleached
all-purpose flour

1 Serrano chile, finely chopped

6 tablespoons truffle oil

In this recipe, a hint of truffle flavor and a bit of spiciness add distinction to the rich, earthy sweetness of roasted beets. This is one of the most beautiful soups we serve at Trout Point, but the brilliant red color will fade with time, so serve it as soon as it's made. If you don't have any truffle oil, don't worry—the soup will be delicious without it.

1. Preheat the oven to 500° F.

2. Place the beets in a glass or ceramic baking dish, cover, and roast until they are soft to the touch of a fork, about 30 minutes. When cool enough to handle, peel, and remove stems and roots.

3. Combine the Mushroom Stock with 3½ cups of the chicken stock in a medium saucepan, and heat over medium heat.

4. While the stock is heating, heat the olive oil in a large skillet. Add the garlic and chiles, and sauté until the garlic is browned but not crisped, about 5 minutes. Add the onion, bell pepper, caraway seeds, and the freshly ground black pepper, and sauté until the onion has caramelized, about 10 minutes.

5. Stir the flour into the vegetable mixture. When the flour has been incorporated, add the remaining ½ cup stock, and mix well.

6. Add this mixture to the heated stock in the saucepan.

7. Transfer three-fourths of the roasted beets to a blender, and puree. Coarsely chop the remaining beets. Add the beat puree to the stock mixture and mix thoroughly. Add the chopped

beets and Serrano chile and bring to a simmer. Ladle the soup into individual bowls, and sprinkle 1 tablespoon of the truffle oil across the top of each serving. Serve immediately.

Mushroom Stock

MAKES ABOUT 2 QUARTS

½ cup olive oil

2 onions coarsely chopped

I leek (white and light green
   parts), well rinsed and
   coarsely chopped

4 celery stalks

2 carrots

10 garlic cloves, coarsely
   chopped

I cup dry white wine or dry
   vermouth

I teaspoon dried marjoram
   leaves, or I tablespoon fresh

8 cups mushroom pieces
   (white button, portobello,
   shiitake, porcini, and/or any
   other wild mushrooms),
   stems and caps

1. Heat the olive oil in a large stockpot over medium heat. Add the onions, leek, celery, carrots, and garlic, and sauté until the onions are just starting to caramelize, about 10 minutes.

2. Add the wine to the vegetables. Then add the marjoram and the mushroom pieces and sauté for 5 minutes.

3. Add 6 quarts water to the pot and bring quickly to a boil. Reduce the heat to a simmer, and skim off any scum that forms on the surface. Simmer until the stock is reduced by half, about 2 hours.

4. Strain the stock, and allow it to cool; then cover and refrigerate. It will keep up to 1 week in the refrigerator or up to 2 months in the freezer.

Roasting Vegetables

Roasting vegetables in the oven works especially well when making soups. Roasting develops a supple texture, and vegetables with lots of internal sugar such as beets, turnips, and onions become sweeter, as roasting helps express the sugar. Roasting also deepens the flavors of vegetables such as eggplant. We prefer to roast vegetables whole with the skin on, often rubbing them with a light layer of olive oil before putting them in the oven. We use a hot oven—normally 450° F to 475° F—and then cool and peel the vegetables before using to make soup. Roasting can thus be done several hours beforehand.

Chilled Fava Soup

6 cups fresh fava beans, shelled

½ cup plus 2 tablespoons fresh lemon juice

2 tablespoons extra virgin olive oil

1¼ teaspoons ground cumin

1½ medium tomatoes, pureed

¼ cup chopped fresh flat-leaf parsley

2 tablespoons chopped fresh mint

2 cups heavy cream

1 cup Crème Fraîche (recipe follows)

We grow fava beans, a fantastic Mediterranean ingredient, in the Lodge garden. This thick soup can also be used as a dip or as a spread for bread or crackers.

1. Bring a large pot of salted water to a boil, add the fava beans, and cook for 30 seconds. Drain, and rinse under cold water.
2. Place the beans in a food processor, and process to a paste.
3. Transfer the paste to a large mixing bowl, and stir in the lemon juice and olive oil until smooth. Add the cumin, tomatoes, parsley, mint, and cream. Stir well. Cover and chill in the refrigerator for at least 1 hour, or as long as 24 hours.
4. Serve cold, with a dollop of Crème Fraîche on top of each serving.

Crème Fraîche

1 cup heavy cream

2 tablespoons buttermilk, as fresh as possible

Mix the cream and buttermilk together in a small bowl or jar, and cover loosely with plastic wrap. Place in a warm spot and leave for about 8 hours. The mixture should be quite thick, but it can take as long as 24 hours for the crème fraîche to form. Once it is very thick, cover tightly and refrigerate for up to 10 days.

Chilled Blueberry Soup

1 pound blueberries

3 tablespoons unsalted butter

2 tablespoons unbleached
   all-purpose flour

4½ cups Vegetable Stock
   (page 55)

Pinch of ground allspice

Salt and freshly ground black
   pepper

1 cup heavy cream, optional

When fresh wild blueberries appear in the woods, we scurry to collect as much of this delicacy as possible, as it often marks the end of summer. We usually serve this as a lunch soup on warmer days.

1. Remove any stems from the blueberries. Rinse them in a colander, and pat dry.

2. Place the blueberries in a blender or food processor, and puree.

3. Melt the butter in a medium saucepan over medium heat. Add the flour and Vegetable Stock, and stir until well combined. Add the blueberry puree and the allspice, bring to a simmer, and lower the heat. Season to taste with salt and pepper. Add up to 1 cup of the cream, according to your preference. Immediately pour the soup into a large bowl, cover, and chill for at least 1 hour. Serve cold. The soup will keep up to 4 days in the refrigerator.

Grilled Zucchini and Blue Cheese Soup

4 medium zucchini

2 tablespoons extra virgin olive oil, plus extra for the zucchini

2 small onions, finely chopped

1 green bell pepper, chopped

4 tablespoons (½ stick) unsalted butter

⅓ cup unbleached all-purpose flour

2 cups Vegetable Stock (page 55)

3 tablespoons Asian fish sauce, optional (see page 61)

½ cup heavy cream

4 ounces high-quality cow's-milk blue cheese, such as Stilton, crumbled

For this recipe, you can use zucchini of any shape or color. Grilling the zucchini lends plenty of flavor to the soup, and it is well complemented by the richness of the blue cheese.

1. Heat an indoor grill pan over medium-high heat. Rub the zucchini with olive oil and grill them, turning them frequently, until well charred, 8 to 10 minutes. Set aside.

2. Heat the 2 tablespoons olive oil in a medium saucepan over medium heat. Add the onions and bell pepper, and sauté until softened, 5 minutes.

3. Add the butter and stir until it's melted. Stir the flour into the vegetables. When the flour has been absorbed, stir in ½ cup of the Vegetable Stock, mixing thoroughly.

4. Transfer the mixture to a blender, add the zucchini, and puree.

5. Combine the zucchini mixture, the remaining 1½ cups stock, and the fish sauce, if using, in the saucepan. Cook for 5 minutes over medium heat.

6. Add the cream and the cheese. Stir, and cook for 1 minute. Serve immediately.

Cashew Chili

8 tablespoons extra virgin
   olive oil

2 white or yellow onions,
   chopped

1½ green bell peppers,
   chopped

2 celery stalks, chopped

4 garlic cloves, finely chopped

This hearty vegetarian recipe is adapted from Cabbage-town Café, one of our favorite restaurants in Ithaca, New York, which is unfortunately now closed. Remember to add the cashews at the last minute, so they retain their crunchy texture. This chili is delicious when topped with grated sharp white Cheddar cheese.

4 cups red kidney beans,
   cooked or canned, drained
6 medium tomatoes, chopped
   or pureed
1½ tablespoons chipotle
   pepper powder, or 1 dried
   chipotle ground to a paste
   with a mortar and pestle
1 cup Vegetable Stock
   (page 55) or Mushroom
   Stock (page 46), or as
   needed
1 bay leaf
1 tablespoon dried oregano
2 teaspoons ground cumin
1½ teaspoons ground turmeric
1 tablespoon Asian fish sauce
   (see page 61)
1 teaspoon cayenne pepper
½ teaspoon white pepper
½ teaspoon dried thyme leaves
1 teaspoon freshly ground
   black pepper
½ teaspoon onion powder
2 teaspoons salt, or to taste
1 cup salted cashew nuts

1. Heat 6 tablespoons of the olive oil in a large saucepan over medium heat. Add the onions, bell peppers, celery, and garlic. Sauté until softened, 5 minutes. Then add the beans, the tomatoes, and the chipotle. Add enough stock to bring the chili to the desired consistency, and bring to a simmer. Add all the remaining ingredients except the cashews.

2. Heat the remaining 2 tablespoons olive oil in a small skillet over medium heat. Add the cashews and toast, tossing frequently, for 5 minutes.

3. Taste the chili for seasoning, and add more stock if needed. Just before serving, stir in the cashews. Serve hot.

Cabbage and Lentil Soup

6 tablespoons extra virgin olive oil

8 garlic cloves, chopped

3 dried red chiles, chopped

2 tablespoons finely chopped onion

¼ cup grated green bell pepper

1 medium tomato, coarsely chopped

2 tablespoons unbleached all-purpose flour

1 small head cabbage, cored and coarsely chopped

2 ounces Salmon Bacon (page 212)

4 cups Seafood Stock (page 65) or Vegetable Stock (recipe follows)

1½ cups dried lentils

2 tablespoons Asian fish sauce (see page 61)

Salt

We serve this filling, warming soup in the colder fall months, while the Lodge guests look out from the dining room at the brilliant colors of the autumn leaves. For a vegetarian option, omit the salmon bacon.

1. Heat 4 tablespoons of the olive oil in a large saucepan over medium heat. Add the garlic and chiles, and sauté until the garlic has browned, 7 to 9 minutes. Raise the heat slightly and add the onion, bell pepper, and tomato. Cook until the onion is transparent and most of the tomato liquid has evaporated, about 5 minutes.

2. Add the flour and incorporate it into the mixture. Then add the cabbage. Reduce the heat to low, cover, and cook until the cabbage is completely soft, stirring and tossing it occasionally, about 10 minutes.

3. Meanwhile, heat the remaining 2 tablespoons olive oil in a small skillet, and sauté the Salmon Bacon over medium-high heat until crisp and fragrant, 4 to 5 minutes. Add the Salmon Bacon and oil to the cabbage mixture.

4. Add the stock to the mixture and bring to a simmer.

5. Transfer the mixture to a blender, and puree.

6. Return the pureed soup to the saucepan and add the lentils. Simmer until the lentils are tender, 12 to 15 minutes.

Just before serving, stir in the fish sauce and salt to taste.

Vegetable Stock

1 tablespoon olive oil

2 medium onions, coarsely
    chopped

3 garlic cloves, chopped

1 fennel bulb, cut in half

1 large leek, top third trimmed
    off, well rinsed

¼ cup dry vermouth

3 carrots

4 celery stalks

3 portobello mushrooms, or
    10 white button mushrooms

1 teaspoon dried thyme leaves

1 tablespoon dried oregano

1. Heat the olive oil in a stockpot over medium heat, and add the onions, garlic, fennel, and leek. Sauté for 8 minutes, or until the onions start to caramelize.

2. Add the vermouth. Then add the carrots, celery, mushrooms, thyme, and oregano. Cook for 5 minutes.

3. Add 8 cups cold water, or enough to cover the ingredients. Bring to a high boil, then lower the heat to a simmer. Cook, skimming any scum off the surface after the first 30 minutes, until reduced to 4 cups, about 1½ hours.

4. Strain the stock and allow it to cool; then cover and refrigerate. The stock will keep for up to 5 days in the refrigerator or up to 1 month in the freezer.

Wild Mushroom Soup

4 tablespoons (½ stick)
　unsalted butter

I onion, chopped

3 garlic cloves, chopped

2 tablespoons chopped green
　bell pepper

I teaspoon chopped celery

I tablespoon chopped fresh
　parsley

¾ cup dried porcini
　mushrooms

3 tablespoons unbleached
　all-purpose flour

2 cups coarsely chopped fresh
　mushrooms (black trumpets,
　chanterelles, portobello,
　or white button)

4 cups Seafood Stock (page
　65) or Vegetable Stock (page
　55)

Salt and freshly ground black
　pepper

As the seasons progress from spring to fall, edible wild mushrooms appear in abundance in the forest surrounding the Lodge. Nova Scotia is home to the black trumpet mushroom, one of the treasured ingredients of French-inspired cooking. Specialty food stores may have black trumpets seasonally; you can also use dried. If the mushrooms listed here are not available, use any other mushrooms you can get your hands on for this delectable soup. It's a tasty treat after coming in from a blustery fall day of picking wild edibles.

1. Heat the butter in a saucepan over medium heat. Add the onion, garlic, bell pepper, celery, parsley, and porcini mushrooms. Sauté for about 6 minutes.

2. Sprinkle the flour over the vegetables, and mix it in thoroughly. Continue to cook, allowing the flour to brown, about 1 minute.

3. Add the fresh mushrooms and cook until softened, about 3 minutes.

4. Add the stock and simmer for 10 minutes. Season with salt and pepper, and serve hot.

Roasted Eggplant Soup

1 eggplant

2 tablespoons extra virgin olive oil

1 cup chopped green bell pepper

1 white onion, chopped

2 tablespoons unbleached all-purpose flour

2 cups Vegetable Stock (page 55)

1 teaspoon sea salt

1 tablespoon ground turmeric

3 red bell peppers, grilled (see page 60), cored, seeded, and sliced

1 tablespoon Asian fish sauce (see page 61)

One 14-ounce can coconut milk

2 tablespoons coarsely chopped fresh basil leaves

A Trout Point favorite, this is eggplant with a distinct Creole twist. The magnificent oven-roasted flavor of the main ingredient blends sensuously with the trinity of bell pepper, onion, and celery. Fresh basil brings a final touch of vitality!

1. Preheat the oven to 400° F.

2. Place the whole eggplant on the oven rack and roast for about 1 hour, or until it is completely soft. Be sure to prick the skin once with a fork after it starts to cook, or the eggplant will explode.

3. Remove the eggplant from the oven, allow it to cool, and then peel off the skin. It should be quite easy to separate the skin from the pulp. Chop the eggplant into large pieces.

4. Heat the olive oil in a medium saucepan over medium heat. Add the green bell pepper and onion, and sauté until the onion becomes translucent, about 5 minutes. Add the flour, mix it in, and cook for 30 seconds. Slowly add the Vegetable Stock and 2 cups water. Then add the roasted eggplant. Simmer for 5 minutes.

5. Transfer any large pieces of eggplant to a blender or food processor, and blend until velvety. Return the puree to the soup. Stir in the salt and turmeric, and add the grilled red pepper slices. Simmer for 10 minutes.

6. Add the fish sauce and coconut milk, stirring to blend. Then add the basil leaves, immediately remove from the heat, and serve.

Saffron Mussel Bisque

1 tablespoon extra virgin olive
    oil

1 red bell pepper, diced

6¼ cups Seafood Stock
    (page 65) or Chicken Stock
    (page 60)

½ cup sultana (golden) raisins

1 large carrot, sliced

2 medium potatoes, diced

Pinch of saffron threads

2 bay leaves

3 tablespoons pure maple
    syrup

3 tablespoons Asian fish sauce
    (see page 61)

1 tablespoon ground turmeric

1 tablespoon fresh lemon juice

30 fresh mussels

½ cup whole milk

One 14-ounce can coconut
    milk

Freshly ground black pepper

¼ cup crushed toasted
    almonds (see page 23)

Our soups usually feature the fresh seafood available that day. Nova Scotia mussels and scallops are unsurpassed. Their flavor is so distinct that this soup often charms guests who have never enjoyed such fresh seafood.

1. Heat the olive oil in a medium saucepan over medium-low heat. Add the bell pepper and sauté until wilted, about 5 minutes. Add the stock, raise the heat, and bring to a boil.

2. Add the sultana raisins, carrot, potatoes, saffron, bay leaves, maple syrup, fish sauce, turmeric, and lemon juice. Reduce the heat and simmer for 30 minutes.

3. Add half of the mussels and simmer until they open, about 4 minutes. Remove the mussels from the soup, remove the meat from the shells, and set the meat aside.

4. Five minutes before serving, add the milk, coconut milk, black pepper, and remaining mussels to the soup. Taste, and if needed, adjust the flavor with more fish sauce and turmeric. Simmer until the mussels open. Remove them from the soup and remove the meat from the shells. Return all the shelled mussels to the soup.

5. Pour the soup into bowls, and top with the crushed almonds. Serve hot.

Chicken Stock

4 tablespoons olive oil

1 large white onion, coarsely chopped

2 garlic cloves, smashed with the side of a knife

4 leeks (white and light green parts), trimmed and cleaned

1 carrot

4 celery stalks, coarsely chopped

1 tablespoon chopped lovage, optional

4 whole cloves

5 sprigs thyme

4 pounds chicken parts (necks, wings, and bones), rinsed

2 teaspoons salt

1. Heat the oil in a large stockpot over medium heat. Add the onion, garlic, leeks, carrot, celery, lovage, if using, cloves, and thyme. Sauté the vegetables until just tender, about 5 minutes.

2. Add the chicken parts and salt, and stir to mix. Add cold water to cover the chicken, about 5 quarts. Bring to a simmer.

3. Simmer the stock, skimming off any impurities that rise to the surface, for about 3 hours, or until reduced to about 2 quarts. Strain the stock through a fine strainer. Allow to cool, and skim off any fat that rises to the surface. The stock will keep tightly sealed in the refrigerator for up to 5 days or in the freezer for up to a month.

Grilled Bell Peppers

Nothing lends better flavor and texture to bell peppers—red, green, or yellow—than char-grilling. This process removes the bitter skin, improves the texture, and enriches the sweetness of the peppers. The skin will bubble and blacken, while the flesh underneath will remain uncharred. To char-grill over an open flame, spear the pepper on a long-handled fork and hold it over the flame, rotating it regularly, until it is blackened all over. To char-grill under a broiler, simply place the pepper directly on the oven rack and broil, turning it regularly, until it is blackened all over. When 95 percent of the skin has become charred, put the pepper in a plastic bag, seal it, and allow the pepper to steam in its own heat for about 10 minutes. Then remove the pepper from the bag. You will be able to easily remove the charred skin by slipping it off with your hands. Holding the pepper under cold running water will facilitate the removal of the skin. Once the skin is removed, core, seed, and chop or slice the pepper as needed.

Asian Fish Sauce

Many of our recipes use fish sauce—a concentrated, fermented, salted fish water common to Southeast Asia—to deepen flavors, lend complexity, and serve as an instant fish stock. Fish sauce, though Asian in its current incarnation, is closely related to the ancient Roman ingredient *garum,* which was made by fermenting fish in a brine solution in the sun for several days. *Garum* constituted much of the basis for interregional commerce in Roman times and was highly prized.

Fish sauce is brown in color and possesses a very strong flavor and a pungent aroma, especially when heated in cooking, but don't worry about these pronounced flavors or odors overwhelming your dish. Fish sauce completes soups and other dishes when added near the end of cooking, and we often splash in this special ingredient at the same time as we add the final seasoning of salt and pepper. We usually use Thai or Vietnamese brands; favorites are one called "Three Crabs" for sauces and "Squid Brand" for cooking. France recently signed an agreement giving Vietnamese fish sauce an *appellation d'origine contrôlée,* or AOC, the same status given to fine wines and cheeses and a culinary high honor. The AOC status is specifically for fish sauce from Phuquoc island in Vietnam.

Shrimp Noodle Soup

5 ounces shrimp

3 tablespoons extra virgin
  olive oil

1½ white onions, chopped

1 green bell pepper, chopped

5 cups Seafood Stock (page 65)

4 dried shiitake mushrooms

1-inch piece of ginger, peeled
  and smashed

2 packets bonito shavings

2 tablespoons Asian fish sauce
  (see page 61)

3 rolls Chinese egg noodles

Salt

Freshly ground black pepper

We use dried Chinese noodles made with quail eggs, shrimp, and shrimp roe for this soup. The noodles are generally available in Chinese food markets.

1. Shell and devein the shrimp, reserving the shells.

2. Bring 5 cups water to a boil in a saucepan, add the shrimp shells, and boil until the liquid is flavorful, at least 20 minutes. Strain the shrimp stock and set it aside.

3. Heat the olive oil in a skillet over medium heat, and add the onions and bell pepper. Sauté until the onions are transparent and the pepper is softened, 5 minutes. Set them aside.

4. Combine the shrimp stock and the Seafood Stock in a stockpot, and bring to a simmer. Add the sautéed onions and peppers. Then add the mushrooms, ginger, bonito, and fish sauce. Simmer for 45 minutes.

5. Strain the stock, discarding the solids, and return it to the heat. Bring to a simmer and add the noodles. Cook for 5 minutes.

6. Using a slotted spoon, divide the noodles evenly among warmed soup bowls. Add the shrimp to the stock and simmer for 2 to 3 minutes, or until they barely cease to be transparent. Add salt and black pepper to taste. Place the shrimp in the bowls with the noodles, add the hot stock, and serve.

Bonito Flakes or Shavings

Bonito shavings can commonly be found in Asian groceries. These flakes of salt-dried tuna add concentrated flavor to stocks and soups, only requiring small amounts—an ounce or two—to achieve delicious results. The flakes should be removed from the soup before serving.

Shrimp and Asparagus Soup

1 pound shrimp

8 ounces fresh asparagus

2 tablespoons extra virgin
olive oil

2 garlic cloves

6 dried red chiles, such as
pepperoncino

3 tablespoons Asian fish sauce
(see page 61)

1 teaspoon fresh winter savory

The marriage of shrimp and asparagus makes for an enchanting soup that we often serve in September, lending its warmth just as a hint of cooler weather begins to appear at night. If you are using frozen shrimp, buy them in their shells. Defrost them slowly, and do not let them warm up to room temperature, as shrimp are very delicate and prone to losing their delicate flavor. Always use shrimp shells (and heads if you have them) to make stock for extra flavor, as we do in this dish.

1. Shell and devein the shrimp, reserving the shells.

2. Trim the asparagus, cutting the stems into 2-inch lengths and setting the tender tips aside.

3. Bring 4 cups water to a boil in a saucepan, add the shrimp shells, and boil until flavorful, at least 15 minutes. Strain the shrimp stock and set it aside.

4. Heat the olive oil in a medium saucepan over medium heat. Add the garlic and dried chiles, and sauté until the garlic has softened, about 5 minutes.

5. Add the shrimp stock and bring to a simmer. Add the asparagus stems, and cook until tender, about 4 minutes.

6. Transfer the ingredients to a blender, and blend together. Return the soup to the saucepan and add the asparagus tips and fish sauce. Cook for 5 minutes.

7. Add the shrimp and savory and cook for another 2 to 3 minutes, or until the shrimp are fully cooked. Serve hot.

Smoked Salmon Chowder

2 tablespoons safflower or
   sunflower oil

2 medium onions, chopped

4 garlic cloves, chopped

3 ounces smoked salmon or
   Salmon Bacon (page 212)

1 large potato, cubed

4 tablespoons (½ stick) butter

4 cups Seafood Stock (recipe
   follows)

1 cup heavy cream

12 fresh scallops

Salt

Smoked salmon, a different choice from the usual bacon, imparts a rich, clean flavor to this chowder and eliminates the need to add more seafood. Frying the salmon (or Salmon Bacon, if you have it) is a simple technique for enhancing the soup—it causes the salmon to release its enticing, deep flavors.

1. Heat the oil in a medium saucepan over medium heat. Add the onions and garlic, and sauté until the onions are caramelized, 8 to 10 minutes. Add the salmon and sauté until it is crisp and fragrant, about 4 minutes. It's fine if it crumbles, but do not let it burn.

2. Add the potato and butter, lower the heat, and cook until the potato is tender, about 10 minutes. Add the stock.

3. Add the cream and simmer for 3 minutes. Then add the scallops and cook for another 3 minutes. Season with salt, and serve.

Seafood Stock

1 tablespoon olive oil

1 onion, coarsely chopped

1 large leek, top third trimmed off, well rinsed

3 garlic cloves, chopped

2 celery stalks

2 pounds fish bones, fish heads (gills removed), shrimp shells, whole oysters or mussels

1. Heat the olive oil in a stockpot over medium heat. Add the onion, leek, garlic, and celery. Sauté for 8 minutes, or until the onion starts to caramelize.

2. Add the seafood and any juices. Immediately add 8 cups cold water, or more as needed to cover all the ingredients. Bring to a high boil, then lower the heat to a simmer. Cook, skimming the surface at least once after the first 30 minutes, until reduced to 1 quart, about 2 hours.

3. Strain the stock and allow it to cool. The stock will keep in the refrigerator for up to 4 days and in the freezer for 1 month.

Potato and Smoked Salmon Soup

4 tablespoons (½ stick)
   unsalted butter

2 ounces smoked salmon, in
   large pieces

1 onion, chopped

2 tablespoons chopped celery

2 cloves garlic, chopped

1 tablespoon chopped fresh
   flat-leaf parsley

2 tablespoons unbleached
   all-purpose flour

4 cups Seafood Stock
   (page 65)

6 small new potatoes, cut into
   ½-inch cubes

1 carrot, chopped

Salt and freshly ground black
   pepper

"But many times the Savages living near us have caught some quantity of Sturgeon, Salmon, or meals of fish. . . ."

—Marc Lescarbot,
Histoire de la Nouvelle-France, 1609

An excellent soup with lots of flavor, but none of the cream found the preceding chowder, this may be served hot or cold.

1. Melt the butter in a medium skillet over medium heat. Add the salmon, onion, celery, garlic, and parsley, and sauté until fragrant, 3 to 4 minutes.

2. Stir in the flour. When the flour begins to cake, add the Seafood Stock and bring the mixture to a simmer.

3. Add the potatoes, carrot, and salt and pepper to taste. Cook until the vegetables are tender, about 10 minutes. Serve hot or chilled.

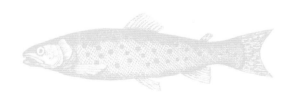

Soup of Salt Cod with Orange-Cured Olives

SERVES 6

½ cup small pieces salt cod
(1 to 1½ inches)

4 cups Seafood Stock
(page 65)

1 tablespoon peanut oil

1 large onion, halved and
thinly sliced

2 tablespoons unbleached
all-purpose flour

1 tablespoon unsalted butter

10 green orange-cured olives,
pitted and sliced, brine
reserved

1 teaspoon Asian fish sauce
(see page 61)

1 tablespoon chopped fresh
cilantro leaves

Although *bacalao* (dried salt cod) is often associated with the Mediterranean, the best codfish actually comes from the North Atlantic waters off Nova Scotia and Newfoundland. Salt cod constitutes as much a part of Acadian French cuisine in the North Atlantic as it has for centuries in Portugal, Spain, and Italy. Many recipes call for soaking the salt cod in water for twenty-four hours or longer, but excessive soaking can drain away as much flavor as salt. Try soaking the cod for just ten to twelve hours, and remember not to add any additional salt to the dish you are preparing. Here, we are using small pieces of salt cod that require only a brief soaking. The addition of green olives that have been cured and marinated with orange rind lends a further Mediterranean touch to a very local ingredient.

1. Soak the salt cod in cold water to cover for 15 minutes, then drain. Repeat this three more times. Set it aside to drain.

2. Pour the stock into a saucepan and bring it to a simmer.

3. Meanwhile, heat the peanut oil in a skillet over medium heat. Add the onion and sauté, gradually adding the salt cod pieces, until the onion is caramelized, 8 to 10 minutes. Then add the flour, mixing it in well. Add the butter and stir until it has melted.

4. Add the cod mixture to the simmering stock. Add the olives, 1 tablespoon of the reserved olive brine, and the fish sauce. Cook for 2 minutes.

5. Add the cilantro and simmer for 5 minutes. Serve hot.

Leek Soup with Potato-Scallop Dumplings

For the dumplings

8 ounces fresh scallops

8 ounces (1 cup) mashed
  potatoes

½ cup finely chopped onion

½ cup finely chopped green
  bell pepper

½ cup grated Parmigiano-
  Reggiano cheese

Grated zest of 1 lemon

Salt and freshly ground black
  pepper

For the soup

2 tablespoons extra virgin
  olive oil or peanut oil

3 leeks (white and light green
  parts), well rinsed and
  chopped

3 tablespoons Asian fish sauce
  (see page 61)

1 teaspoon freshly ground
  black pepper

6 cups Seafood Stock
  (page 65)

Leeks and potatoes have great affinity of flavors. While the classic French vichyssoise is the consummate combination, our leek soup with potato-scallop dumplings takes this affinity one step further by combining these natural allies with a savory fish stock and sweet scallops. This is also a great way to use up leftover mashed potatoes.

Prepare the dumplings

1. Finely chop the scallops. In a mixing bowl, combine the scallops thoroughly with all the other dumpling ingredients. Set aside.

Make the soup

2. Heat the olive oil over medium heat in a medium saucepan or small stockpot. Add the leeks and sauté until they wilt, about 10 minutes. Stir in the fish sauce and pepper. Add the Seafood Stock and bring to a simmer.

3. Taste the soup and adjust for salt and seasoning. Drop rounded tablespoons of the dumpling mixture into the simmering soup, and cook for 1 minute. Serve immediately.

Crawfish Bisque

8 tablespoons (1 stick)
   unsalted butter

1½ cups chopped onions

½ cup chopped green bell
   pepper

½ cup chopped celery

1 tomato, chopped

1 tablespoon chopped fresh
   flat-leaf parsley

2½ cups Chicken Stock (page
   60), Mushroom Stock
   (page 46), or Vegetable
   Stock (page 55)

¼ cup sweet sherry

1 teaspoon sugar

½ teaspoon sea salt

1 tablespoon fresh lime juice

¼ teaspoon ground cloves

¼ teaspoon ground mace

1 teaspoon dried thyme leaves

½ cup heavy cream

1 pound peeled crawfish tails

A bisque is a thick, creamy soup, usually containing seafood, best represented in Louisiana cuisine by crawfish bisque. Crawfish, also known as crayfish, are a staple of Louisiana cuisine, though they are also eaten throughout parts of Europe and Asia. These small crustaceans have meaty tails and are usually cooked whole with their shells on, though these days you can also find good quality shelled frozen tails in specialty stores or by mail order. Like lobster, they turn red when cooked, and have sweet, juicy meat. Traditionally crawfish bisque was made the same day a family boiled crawfish—when there were plenty of relatives around to help peel the boiled crawfish and clean the head and body shells. Those shells were then stuffed with crawfish forcemeat (a forcemeat is composed of minced meat, often combined with other ingredients, that can be spread and shaped) and served in the bisque. Since fresh crawfish—and crawfish-experienced relatives—are not available at Trout Point, we prepare this equally tasty version without the stuffed shells.

1. Heat the butter in a medium saucepan over medium heat. Add the onions, bell peppers, celery, tomatoes, and parsley, and sauté until the onions soften and become translucent, about 7 minutes. Add the stock and bring to a simmer.

2. Transfer the mixture to a blender, and puree. Return the puree to the saucepan and stir in the sherry, sugar, salt, lime juice, cloves, mace, and thyme. Simmer for 20 minutes. Add the cream and cook for 3 minutes.

3. Add the crawfish, cook for 1 minute, and serve immediately.

Chapter three

Wild Foods

For there was no one who, two days before his turn came, failed to go hunting or fishing, and to bring back some delicacy in addition to our ordinary fare.

—Marc Lescarbot, describing the Order of Good Cheer in
Histoire de la Nouvelle-France, 1609

The natural world surrounding the Great Lodge always has a distinctive and honored place in our cooking, as we regularly include "wild foods" on the daily menu. Trout Point Lodge looks out to the Tusket River, the centerpiece of a twenty-mile-wide watershed basin that includes more than 310 miles of indented and stunningly beautiful coastline. The salt marshes of the Tusket River Basin cover an astounding eight thousand acres and form a rich environment and inviting meeting place between the inland boreal forest and the open ocean. We comb through forest, field, and marsh all over the county, looking for seasonal wild delicacies.

Yarmouth County and Argyle Municipality, the home of Trout Point Lodge, are made up of almost more water than land. From Wedge Point to Tusket Falls, the estuary is 15 miles in length. From the head of the tide, the Great Tusket River reaches inland for 58 miles, originating at Long Tusket Lake. The main river and its ten branches or forks stretch a total of 220 miles, draining 167 lakes and countless brooks, including Trout Point's own two lakes. All the rivers and brooks of the entire watershed drain an even greater number of 213 lakes. This fabulous world of water, marsh, and woods is as inviting to the wild-food forager today as it was in 1605, and we've gathered together a few recipes that make use of this natural abundance. You can find most of these plants, mushrooms, and shellfish throughout North America.

Fiddlehead Ferns

2 tablespoons extra virgin
olive oil

3 garlic cloves, chopped

2 dried hot red peppers, such
as cayenne or pepperoncino,
crushed or flaked, or dried
red pepper flakes

8 ounces fresh fiddlehead
ferns, soaked in water for
30 minutes and rinsed

1 teaspoon salt, or to taste

½ teaspoon freshly ground
black pepper

This bountiful early spring crop can often be found in specialty food stores. A simple treatment with a bit of hot pepper and garlic is all that's needed to bring out the delicious, asparagus-like flavor of the fiddleheads. To clean these small furled ferns, soak them in water, rinse well, and pick off as much of the papery brown chaff as possible.

1. Heat the olive oil in a large skillet over low heat. Add the garlic and peppers, and sauté until the garlic caramelizes and the peppers become toasted, about 8 minutes. Toss in the whole fiddlehead ferns, coating them with the oil. Cook for 3 to 5 minutes, until the fiddleheads begin to wilt and change color. Add the salt and black pepper.

2. Remove from the heat and serve.

Sweet Fern

We find this dense, deep green fern in abundance along the edges of country roads near Trout Point, and more sparingly in the forest interior, from the beginning of July to the end of summer. Its most notable characteristics are its sweet, pungent smell and its small burrs, or fruits, which are usually a lighter green than the leaves. Sweet ferns go very well with scallops. Try the recipe for Spicy Cornmeal-Crusted Scallops with Wild Sweet Fern Butter on page 129.

Cattail and Narrow-Leafed Cattail

Everyone knows what cattail is. These large decorative plants stand tall in gullies along the highway and on the edges of ponds and swamps year-round almost everywhere in North America. The bottom foot of the upright stock is a traditional Native American delicacy. More intriguing is the tender root, or rhizome, that runs underneath the moist earth. The soft, smooth pointed ends of these roots have a clean texture and taste of chicken when grilled. Try serving cattail roots with Cornmeal-Crusted Oyster Mushrooms (page 11).

Lime-Grilled Cattail Root

SERVES 8 AS AN APPETIZER OR SIDE DISH

Juice of 1 lime

1 teaspoon sea salt

½ teaspoon cracked black pepper

¼ cup extra virgin olive oil

16 cattail root ends

Cattail roots have a soft initial flavor that turns into a spicy aftertaste. We like to grill them with a little lime juice and black pepper, not wanting to mask the nutty flavors.

1. Combine the lime juice, salt, pepper, and olive oil in a medium stainless steel or glass bowl, and whisk together to form an emulsion. Add the cattail root ends and marinate them in the lime vinaigrette for 10 minutes.

2. Heat an indoor grill pan over high heat.

3. Remove the cattail roots from the marinade and grill, turning once, until golden brown, 15 seconds each. Serve immediately.

Mussels Cooked in Pine Needles

SERVES 6

2 pounds fresh mussels,
cleaned and debearded

About 2 armfuls clean dry pine
or other conifer needles

A meal featured in a Canadian Broadcasting Corporation program about the Order of Good Cheer inspired us to perfect the settlers' technique of cooking wild-harvested mussels in dry pine and spruce needles. The flavor of the mussels is marvelous—just be careful not to get ashes on them! This is best done in a fireplace or outdoors on a grill.

Arrange a substantial bed of pine needles on the floor of a fireplace or grill. Lay the mussels on the pine needles in a single layer, with at least ½ inch between mussels. To help prevent ashes from getting into the mussels, place a piece of fine-mesh metal hardware cloth or screen over the mussels. Then cover the mussels with pine needles. Ignite the needles at several points around the perimeter, adding more as needed to keep the fire going until the mussels open, 5 to 8 minutes. Pick the mussels out of the ashes and serve immediately.

Yellow Water Lily Leaves Stuffed with Purple Rice

SERVES 8

8 boneless, skinless chicken
thighs, finely chopped

2 onions, finely chopped

2 green bell peppers, finely
chopped

¼ cup unbleached all-purpose
flour

2 eggs, beaten

2 teaspoons coarsely ground
black pepper

2 teaspoons salt

1 teaspoon ground allspice

The water lily—readily found in quiet freshwater lakes, ponds, and rivers during the summer—is one of the most useful of the gourmet wild edibles. The leaves of this fairy-tale plant serve here as an outer wrapper, much as a lotus leaf does. Sautéed, the leaves lose their raw, bitter flavor and blend harmoniously with the spicy rice stuffing. Vietnamese purple rice is a firm, fragrant rice that adds a beautiful color to dishes such as this. It can be found in most Asian or Chinese grocery stores.

¼ teaspoon ground thyme

¼ teaspoon ground mace

¼ teaspoon grated nutmeg

1 cup Vietnamese purple rice

13 yellow lily leaves: 8 large
   (6 to 7 inches long, 5 inches
   wide) and 5 smaller
   (for lining the skillet)

Peanut oil

2 whole star anise

1. In a large bowl, mix together the chicken pieces, onions, bell peppers, flour, eggs, pepper, salt, allspice, thyme, mace, nutmeg, and rice. Set this stuffing aside.

2. Fill a large saucepan with water, bring it to a near boil, and then remove the pan from the heat. Blanch the lily leaves by submerging them in the hot water for just 4 to 5 seconds on each side. (Any longer and the leaves will shrink. To maintain the form and texture of the dish, you want the leaves to shrink around the stuffing during cooking, not during the blanching process.) Pat the leaves dry.

3. Stuff the 8 large blanched leaves as you would grape leaves: Place 2 heaping teaspoons of the stuffing on the center of the back side of each leaf, and fold the left and right sides in so that the edges are touching. Then fold the bottom of the leaf over the stuffing, and roll the wrap into a small, tight rectangular package.

4. Line the bottom of a medium skillet with the smaller lily leaves, and pour enough peanut oil into the pan to cover the leaves. Heat the oil over medium heat. Add the lily rolls and the star anise pods, and sauté the rolls until the lily leaves and the rice are tender, about 40 minutes.

5. Discard the star anise and serve immediately.

Evening Primrose

Like its name, the evening primrose is elegant and intriguing in appearance and flavor. The leaves' bright red tips make a unique and beautiful salad—younger leaves are tender and less peppery. Larger plants provide a root with deep, peppery undertones, which we use to garnish salads. Collect different sizes of roots for a variety of tastes. To separate the meat from the tough, opaque outer root, boil the peeled root for 15 minutes; then slice it in half and remove the soft dark brown, peppery inner meat.

Beer-Battered Elderberry Flowers

1 bottle (12 ounces) pilsner or
   lager beer

1 cup unbleached all-purpose
   flour

1 teaspoon salt

1 teaspoon freshly ground
   black pepper

½ teaspoon ground coriander

8 large bunches of elderberry
   flowers

1 cup peanut oil

The American, or common, elder grows in most of eastern North American in spring and summer, and its flowers bloom in midsummer. The ripe fruits can be made into jam, juice, and pies. The elegant bundles of flowers are delicate and light, appropriate for making a savory treat or side dish. Try these delicate flower fritters with Spicy Cornmeal-Crusted Scallops with Wild Sweet Fern Butter (page 129).

1. Mix the beer with the flour in a medium bowl. Add the salt, pepper, and coriander, and mix well.

2. Dip the elderberry bunches into the batter so that they are completely covered. Set the flowers on a wire rack, and let the excess batter drip off for 15 seconds.

3. Meanwhile, heat the peanut oil in a large deep sauté pan over medium-high heat until it is hot but not smoking. (The oil is ready when a drop of batter floats on top of the oil.)

4. Fry the batter-covered flowers in the hot oil until golden brown on each side, 4 to 5 minutes total. Serve immediately.

Bullrush Blinis Topped with Salmon, Crème Fraîche, and Beluga Caviar

SERVES 8 AS AN APPETIZER

⅔ cup unbleached all-purpose
flour

⅔ cup bullrush flour (see
page 78)

2¼ tablespoons sugar

1 teaspoon salt

4 tablespoons (½ stick)
unsalted butter

1½ cups whole milk

2 teaspoons active dry yeast

3 eggs, lightly beaten

Peanut oil

4 ounces smoked salmon,
sliced

Crème Fraîche (page 47)

Beluga caviar, or other caviar

We've adapted a traditional blini recipe to use bullrush flour. The herbaceous flavor of the bullrush combines perfectly with smoked salmon and cool Crème Fraîche. A topping of caviar lends a touch of richness and elegance.

1. In a bowl, whisk together the all-purpose flour, bullrush flour, sugar, and salt.

2. Heat the butter and milk in a saucepan until the butter is completely melted. Allow to cool to room temperature. Then add the yeast and let it dissolve.

3. Lightly whisk the milk mixture into the flour mixture until the texture is uniform. Cover the bowl with a cloth or plastic wrap and place it in a warm place in the kitchen. Let the batter rise until the volume has doubled, about 1 hour. Mix it briefly to deflate it, and whisk in the eggs.

4. Place a nonstick skillet over medium-low heat, and add just enough peanut oil to cover the surface in a very thin layer. Spoon the batter in quarter-cup amounts onto the skillet, and cook until bubbles appear and the edges are dry. Flip the blinis with a thin spatula and brown on the other side. Keep the blinis warm while you cook the rest, adding more oil as needed. Top each serving with some smoked salmon, a dollop of Crème Fraîche, and a teaspoon of beluga caviar.

Hard-Stem Bullrush

Bullrush abounds in thick stands along marshy roadsides and moist woodlands. Said to be almost as versatile in its gourmet uses as cattail, the bullrush is best gathered from mid-July to the end of August. Our favorite place to collect this tall, easily harvested plant is the dense and sprawling stand of bullrush on Trout Point Road.

We like to use the plant to make flour, which has an aromatic, herbaceous flavor. Collect bullrush seeds by pulling out the loosely connected seed stems at the top of the plant. While collecting them, shake the seeds lightly to remove any insects. To dry them, spread the seed fronds out on a large baking pan, and dry at 180° F in a convection oven for 2 hours. Separate the seeds by running the plant through two fingers firmly pressed together. Grind the separated seeds with a mortar and pestle, and sift once for a fine texture.

Sole in Wild Sorrel Velouté Sauce

8 tablespoons (1 stick)
  unsalted butter

½ cup unbleached all-purpose
  flour

2 cups Seafood Stock
  (page 65)

¼ cup chopped sheep sorrel
  leaves

¼ teaspoon white pepper

¼ teaspoon sugar

Salt to taste

4 egg yolks

6 tablespoons Crème Fraîche
  (page 47)

6 fresh sole fillets

Béchamel sauce is the basic French white sauce made with milk. Velouté sauce has the same blond roux foundation, but is made with fish or chicken stock. Sorrel grows wild around the Lodge. We enhance our velouté with sorrel and use it to dress grilled fresh fish, such as haddock or sole.

1. Melt the butter in a medium saucepan over medium-low heat. Add the flour gradually, whisking constantly until smooth. Stir in the Seafood Stock and cook the sauce until it thickens, about 5 minutes.

2. Bring a small saucepan of water to a boil, add the sorrel, and blanch for 1 minute. Drain, and rinse under cold running water. Crush the sorrel with your fingers and add it to the sauce mixture. Add the pepper, sugar, and salt.

3. Place the egg yolks and Crème Fraîche in a small saucepan, and slowly add ½ cup of the sauce mixture, stirring constantly. Return this mixture to the larger pan of sauce and heat it over low heat—do not boil.

4. Preheat an indoor grill pan over medium heat. Grill the sole fillets 2 to 3 minutes on each side until opaque and cooked through. Serve the grilled sole with a dollop of sauce on each fillet.

Wild Sorrel

Watch your feet: don't mistake this small arrow-leafed plant for a weed! Found in poor soil and disturbed sites in most areas of North America, sheep sorrel has an acidic bite with a robust lemon flavor. Sorrel adds depth to bland salad greens and complements any delicate whitefish.

Black Trumpet Mushrooms

Deep in the hardwood forests of the Tobeatic Wilderness, along what some believe to be a historic aboriginal trading trail, we discovered this choice mushroom en masse at the tip of a small hill. The three-hour round-trip is worth the hike, as we often find delicious chanterelles alongside the pungent black trumpets. These small black mushrooms are common throughout North America.

Black Trumpets with Scrambled Eggs

SERVES 2

2 tablespoons extra virgin olive oil

I cup fresh black trumpet mushrooms

½ small onion, sliced

¼ teaspoon sea salt

¼ teaspoon freshly ground black pepper

3 eggs, beaten

Serve this with Wild Blackberry Breakfast Clafoutis (page 82) and toasted Tusket Brown Whole-Grain Bread (page 169) for a very special breakfast or brunch.

Heat the olive oil in a nonstick skillet over medium heat. Add the mushrooms, onion, salt, and pepper, and sauté until the black trumpets wilt and the onion is translucent, 7 minutes. Add the eggs and stir lightly until they are slightly moist but not runny, 4 to 5 minutes. Serve.

Indian Cucumber Root

This outstanding vegetable root can be found during the summer months about 1 to 2 inches below the ground in moist forest. The margins of the Tusket River act as a breeding ground for this inconspicuously delicious vegetable, which we commonly use to complement salads. Its beautiful creamy color looks spectacular with dark greens and robust tomatoes. Try serving the roots raw with the Tomato and Tuna Salad with Jerez Sherry Vinegar on page 94.

Wild Blackberry Breakfast Clafoutis

3½ cups fresh blackberries

2 eggs

2 egg yolks

¾ cup heavy cream

¼ cup sugar

1 teaspoon pure vanilla extract

We serve these slightly sweet blackberry clafoutis for breakfast in the summer, when the bushes lining the Trout Point Road are laden with fruit. For other blackberry recipes, see the Desserts chapter.

1. Preheat the oven to 375° F.

2. Butter six 1-cup ovenproof baking dishes. Place ½ cup of the blackberries in each dish (reserving the remainder for garnish).

3. In a medium mixing bowl, blend together the eggs, egg yolks, cream, sugar, and vanilla. Divide the egg mixture among the baking dishes.

4. Bake until the custards puff up and start to turn golden, about 35 minutes. Allow them to cool for 5 minutes, then top each clafouti with a few blackberries, and serve immediately.

Wintergreen Crème Anglaise

1 cup whole milk

1 cup heavy cream

¼ cup sugar

3 teaspoons pure vanilla
extract

8 wintergreen sprigs (3 leaves
per sprig), crumpled and
crushed to release their
flavor, but not chopped

3 egg yolks

This custard sauce is magical when served over Chocolate Gourmandise (page 200) and garnished with wintergreen leaves and berries.

1. Fill a large bowl halfway with ice, and set it aside.

2. Combine the milk, cream, sugar, vanilla, and wintergreen in a medium saucepan over medium heat, and cook, stirring constantly, until the peppermint taste is evident, 20 to 30 minutes. Do not boil or scald the milk.

3. Slowly add a little bit of the hot milk mixture to the egg yolks, whisking constantly. Then return the egg mixture to the saucepan, and simmer over low heat for approximately 10 minutes, or until the cream thickens enough to coat the back of a wooden spoon.

4. Pour the mixture into a stainless steel bowl. Place this bowl in the bowl of ice, and stir the crème anglaise until it is cooled and creamy. Crème anglaise will keep up to 4 days in the refrigerator if it is tightly sealed. If a skin forms on the surface, simply remove it, or strain the sauce before using.

Wintergreen

Local Acadians call this small, unassuming plant "teaberry" because the green leaves and red berries are often used in warm infusions. Teaberry, or wintergreen as it is more formally known, mats the forest floor all year round; both the berries and the leaves have a sweet and pleasing peppermint flavor. The soft-tasting, less bitter young leaves, or those that are lighter in color, are preferable to the mature dark green leaves.

Chapter four

Salads

The Savages, for their part, share their fish and their reed panniers full of grapes, in exchange for which they will have some of our foodstuffs. Sieur de Pointincourt, seeing the grapes beautiful and marvelous, has commanded to his butler to take into the boat some vines so that he will have them near.

—Marc Lescarbot, *Histoire de la Nouvelle-France,* 1609

One of the first things guests see when they drive up to Trout Point is the organic vegetable and herb garden, where we grow a variety of greens, picked fresh for each meal. The garden expands in size every year, generously enriched with kelp compost from the seaside, and we've successfully grown shiny red tomatoes and hot green peppers—a feat for the maritime climate of Nova Scotia. The daily mesclun mix includes freshly picked baby collard greens, chicory, buttercrunch, red romaine, and oak leaf lettuces. Salads also give our guests a chance to enjoy fresh wild greens, roots, and herbs picked in the boreal forests surrounding us, allowing them to experience an almost-lost French culinary tradition followed by both the Acadians in Nova Scotia and the Cajuns in Louisiana.

Endive Salad

8 heads Belgian endive, bases
trimmed

¼ cup extra virgin olive oil

Salt and freshly ground black
pepper

One 8-ounce log aged goat
cheese, such as the French
Sainte-Maure, well ripened
but not gooey

5 tablespoons fruity extra
virgin olive oil

3 tablespoons excellent-
quality red wine vinegar

Food writer Elizabeth David once noted that the secret of cooking Belgian endive is not to braise it with liquid or steam, but to simply coat the heads with butter or olive oil and cook them slowly in a pan or on the grill. While she used butter in the French style, we use extra virgin olive oil—either works well. Here we pair both raw and cooked endive with flavorful cheese and fragrant olive oil for an enticing luncheon salad.

1. Preheat an indoor grill pan.
2. Cut 4 of the endives in half. Coat them with olive oil, and season them with salt and pepper. Grill the endives over medium-high heat, turning them once or twice, until they are fully cooked but not mushy, about 15 minutes in total. Set them aside and allow them to cool completely.
3. Cut the cheese into ¼-inch-thick disks. Cut the remaining endives in half.
4. Arrange 2 grilled endive halves around the edge of each plate, and place a raw endive half inside each grilled half. Fan out the cheese disks, about 3 or 4 per plate. Drizzle the fruity olive oil and the wine vinegar over everything, and serve.

Clementine and Black Olive Salad

¼ cup extra virgin olive oil,
plus extra for the spinach

3 tablespoons rice wine
vinegar

Clementines have been a Nova Scotia favorite since the days when sailing ships traded with Europe and the Caribbean. We use them here with another superlative Mediterranean-trade commodity: olives.

¾ cup fine-quality black
  olives, such as Kalamata,
  pitted and sliced in half
4 clementines, peeled and
  separated into sections
2 cups loosely packed baby
  spinach leaves
Salt and freshly ground black
  pepper

1. In a medium bowl, slowly whisk the ¼ cup olive oil into the vinegar until emulsified. Toss in the olives and clementines, and coat them with the dressing.

2. Arrange the baby spinach leaves around the edge of each plate, and place the clementines and olives in the center.

3. Drizzle the spinach with a little extra olive oil. Season with salt and pepper, and serve.

Creole Celery Root Salad

SERVES 6

3 medium leeks (white and
  light green parts), well rinsed
2 medium celery roots, very
  finely sliced
Juice of 1 lemon
½ cup mayonnaise
¼ cup fruity extra virgin olive
  oil
1 plump garlic clove, minced
1 tablespoon chopped fresh
  flat-leaf parsley
3 tablespoons Creole mustard
  or whole-grain mustard
¼ teaspoon dried thyme leaves
¼ teaspoon cayenne pepper
¼ teaspoon white pepper
Salt and freshly ground black
  pepper

Trout Point's variation on the classic New Orleans rémoulade dressing is a robust counterpoint to the savory flavor and resilient texture of fresh celery root.

1. Bring a pot of salted water to a boil, add the leeks, and cook until just tender, about 5 minutes. Drain and allow to cool. Slice the leeks, and mix them with the celery root and lemon juice in a bowl.

2. In a separate bowl, thoroughly blend together the mayonnaise, olive oil, garlic, parsley, mustard, thyme, cayenne, and white pepper.

3. Coat the celery root mixture with this dressing, season with salt and pepper, cover, and refrigerate for 1 hour before serving.

Artichoke and Fresh Herb Salad

For the salad

Juice of 1 lemon

4 artichokes, trimmed

2 tablespoons olive oil

4 button mushrooms

1 medium Spanish onion,
   finely chopped

3 scallions (white and light
   green parts), finely sliced

1 celery stalk, chopped

1 cup grated Parmigiano-
   Reggiano cheese

For the dressing

6 tablespoons rice wine
   vinegar

1 garlic clove, minced

½ teaspoon Creole mustard or
   whole-grain mustard

½ teaspoon grated lemon zest

1 teaspoon chopped fresh basil

1 teaspoon chopped fresh flat-
   leaf parsley

1 teaspoon chopped fresh
   thyme

½ cup extra virgin olive oil

Artichokes are a favorite food of southern Louisiana, a tradition clearly shared with our Spanish and French forebears. You can store this salad for up to two days in the refrigerator.

1. Bring a large pot of lightly salted water to a boil, and add the lemon juice. Add the artichokes and cook at a gentle boil until tender, 30 minutes.

2. While the artichokes are cooking, heat the olive oil in a small skillet. Add the mushrooms and sauté until tender, 7 minutes. Then coarsely chop the mushrooms and set them aside.

3. Drain the artichokes. When they are cool enough to handle, remove all the leaves, reserving a few of the tender inner leaves. Trim off and discard the stem and the choke. Chop the artichoke bottoms.

4. In a large bowl, toss the artichoke bottoms with the mushrooms, onion, scallions, celery, and cheese.

5. In small bowl, combine all the dressing ingredients except the olive oil. Gradually add the oil, whisking until emulsified. Add the dressing to the salad and toss well. Garnish the salad with the reserved artichoke leaves, and serve.

Arugula Salad with Baby Squid

¼ cup unbleached all-purpose
  flour

1 teaspoon salt

1 teaspoon freshly ground
  black pepper

2 teaspoons herbes de
  Provence

1 cup loosely packed fresh
  arugula leaves

½ red bell pepper, cut into
  large dice

2 canned hearts of palm,
  sliced into ½-inch rounds
  (½ cup)

Peanut or vegetable oil

16 baby squid, cleaned,
  with the tentacles stuffed
  into the hollow cavity of
  the bodies

Creamy Herb Dressing
  (page 98)

¼ cup grated aged Manchego
  or Parmigiano-Reggiano
  cheese

Cold salads featuring fresh seafood can be easily prepared and elegantly presented. A large salad is a meal in
itself, and a smaller salad is an inviting first course.

1. Stir the flour, salt, pepper, and herbes de Provence together on a plate. Set it aside.

2. Divide the arugula among four plates, mounding it in the
center, and scatter the bell pepper over it. Arrange the hearts
of palm on top, and set the plates aside.

3. Pour oil to a depth of 2 inches in a deep, heavy sauté pan,
and heat it over medium-high heat until it is very hot but not
smoking.

4. Dredge the squid in the flour mixture, shaking off any excess. Fry the squid in the hot oil until they start to crisp,
about 4 minutes.

5. Arrange four squid around each salad, and dress with the
Creamy Herb Dressing. Top with the grated cheese and
serve.

Cleaning Squid

Rinse the squid in cold water. Insert your index finger into the body cavity and locate the feather (spine) of the squid, pulling it straight out without breaking it. If the feather breaks, simply ensure that you remove all the pieces, which are made of translucent cartilage. Next, remove all interior body parts and white-colored fat from the cavity, rinsing the squid thoroughly with cold water until the interior cavity is perfectly clean. Cut the tentacles from the body at the point directly in front of the eyes where they attach to the body.

Grilled Baby Squid and Vegetable Salad

SERVES 4

2 pounds whole baby squid

4 garlic cloves, chopped

½ cup extra virgin olive oil, plus more for dressing the salad

2 long sweet green chile peppers

Salt and freshly ground black pepper

4 heads Belgian endive, halved lengthwise

2 long white onions, halved lengthwise (if you can't find long onions, use round ones)

Baby squid and octopus make terrific room-temperature salads, ideal to serve on a day when you don't want to do too much cooking. You can make this salad up to two hours in advance and serve it whenever your guests are hungry. The flavor of the vegetables is greatly enhanced by the grilling. A crisp white wine, like a Spanish Rueda or an Oregon Sauvignon Blanc, will complement these flavors.

1. Preheat an indoor grill pan until hot.
2. Clean the squid. Cut off the tentacles just above the point where are attached to the body.
3. Mix the squid, the chopped garlic, and ¼ cup of the olive oil in a small bowl. Set it aside.
4. Cut the peppers in half crosswise, and then into quarters lengthwise. Pour the remaining ¼ cup olive oil onto a plate and sprinkle it liberally with salt

and pepper. Coat the endives, peppers, and onions thoroughly with the seasoned olive oil.

5. Grill the endives and the onions, turning them periodically, over medium-high heat, until soft, 12 to 14 minutes. Pay particular attention to the endives: each half should be cooked through and soft but still hold together, with the outer leaves browned. Transfer the endives and onions to a plate and set it aside.

6. Grill the pepper pieces until they are soft and starting to char, 10 minutes. Add the squid and cook until just done, 1 to 1½ minutes. Transfer the peppers and squid to the plate containing the other ingredients. When they have cooled, cut the pepper pieces into narrow strips.

7. Arrange the vegetables and squid decoratively on a platter or individual plates, and drizzle with olive oil. Sprinkle salt on the squid, and pour any collected juices over the salad. Serve at room temperature.

Lobster Potato Salad

SERVES 6

6 medium red potatoes, scrubbed

6 eggs

¼ cup plus 2 tablespoons mayonnaise

2 tablespoons Creole mustard or whole-grain mustard

½ teaspoon cayenne pepper, or to taste

Salt

3 pounds cooked lobster meat, coarsely chopped

Homemade potato salad is traditionally enjoyed alongside fresh gumbo. We've used fresh Nova Scotia lobster meat in this sumptuous version.

1. Bring a large saucepan of lightly salted water to boil. Add the potatoes and boil until the potatoes are tender and can easily be pierced with a fork. Drain and allow the potatoes to cool. Cut into cubes.

2. Bring another large saucepan of water to a boil. Add the eggs and boil 8 minutes, until hard. Remove the eggs from the water and allow to cool.

3. Remove the shells from the eggs. Slice the eggs in half and separate the egg whites from the egg yolks. Coarsely chop the whites and set aside. Place the

egg yolks in a medium bowl and add the mayonnaise, mustard, and cayenne pepper. Mash the ingredients together until the mixture is smooth. Add salt to taste.

4. Add the lobster meat, potatoes, and the egg whites to the egg yolk mixture. Mix well. Chill before serving.

Sea Bean and Mussel Salad

SERVES 4

1 cup dry white wine

4 garlic cloves: 3 smashed with the side of a knife, 1 minced

2 tablespoons minced celery

2 tablespoons minced red bell pepper

1 small onion, thinly sliced

1 bay leaf

2 pounds fresh mussels, cleaned and debearded

2 tablespoons white wine vinegar

2 teaspoons minced fresh tarragon

½ teaspoon Dijon mustard

¼ cup extra virgin olive oil

Salt and freshly ground black pepper

8 ounces sea beans, soaked in cool water for 30 minutes and drained

2 cups shredded romaine lettuce

Sea beans, also known as marsh samphire or glasswort, grow in the tidal marshes along the Pacific and Atlantic coasts. In Nova Scotia, we stop to pick sea beans on our way toward the rich mussel beds of the Chebogue River. By the time we get back to the Lodge, we have a complete dish gathered from nature. Sea beans have crisp, succulent leaves and stems with a briny taste that perfectly complements the mussels' sweetness. They're now commonly available in quality supermarkets and specialty stores around North America.

1. In a medium saucepan, combine the wine, smashed garlic cloves, celery, bell pepper, onion, and bay leaf, and bring to a boil. Reduce the heat, cover, and simmer for 3 minutes.

2. Add the mussels, cover, and cook over high heat until they open, 3 to 5 minutes. Transfer the mussels to a bowl, discarding any that do not open. Remove the meat from the shells and place it in a bowl.

3. Whisk the vinegar, tarragon, mustard, and minced garlic together in a small bowl. Slowly add the olive oil, whisking until emulsified. Season with salt and pepper.

4. Add the sea beans to the mussels and toss with 3 tablespoons of the vinaigrette. Season with salt and pepper. Toss the romaine with the remaining vinaigrette and mound it on four plates. Top with the mussel salad, and serve.

No Sea Beans?

If you can't locate sea beans, it's worth making this salad with slender green beans instead. Simply blanch the beans in the strained mussel-cooking liquid until they are bright green and tender, about 2 minutes. Remove them with a slotted spoon, pat them dry, and let them cool completely. Then cut the beans into 1½-inch lengths.

2 medium red tomatoes, thinly sliced

2 medium yellow tomatoes, thinly sliced

2 medium orange tomatoes, thinly sliced

2 tablespoons Jerez sherry vinegar

2 tablespoons extra virgin olive oil

1 teaspoon sea salt

6 ounces good-quality canned or jarred tuna, such as bonito (available in specialty stores), drained and left in large chunks

Cracked black pepper

Tomato and Tuna Salad with Jerez Sherry Vinegar

SERVES 4

We grow as many different kinds of tomatoes as we can. This salad works spectacularly if you can get yellow, orange, and red varieties of about the same size. If not, simply use plump, flavorful red ones. The distinctive flavor of Spanish Jerez sherry vinegar blends sumptuously with tomatoes and tuna.

1. Arrange the tomatoes slices decoratively on four plates, alternating colors.

2. In a small mixing bowl, whisk the vinegar and oil together until emulsified. Sprinkle the salt over the tomatoes, and then pour the dressing over them. Allow the tomatoes to marinate for at least 30 minutes.

3. Top the tomatoes with chunks of tuna and a sprinkling of black pepper. Serve.

Emulsions

To "emulsify" means to blend together two liquids that, under normal circumstances, do not mix, such as oil and vinegar. To create an emulsion, slowly add one liquid to the other while whisking, agitating, or using an electric blender or food processor. Many salad dressings are emulsions containing oil. Other examples include sauces such as hollandaise and mayonnaise. Many emulsions are unstable, and will separate given some time. In an emulsion, droplets of one liquid are literally broken up and distributed throughout the other, thus making the mixture satiny in appearance and texture.

Dressings

Lemon-Honey Vinaigrette

MAKES ABOUT ¾ cup

Juice of 1 lemon

2 tablespoons wildflower
honey

½ cup extra virgin olive oil

Spoon this over a salad of bitter or spicy greens, such as chicory and radicchio, or arugula.

Whisk the lemon juice and honey together in a small bowl. Gradually add the olive oil, whisking until emulsified. The vinaigrette will keep in an airtight container in the refrigerator for up to 1 week.

Raspberry Vinaigrette

MAKES ABOUT ½ CUP

2 tablespoons raspberry syrup

3 tablespoons balsamic
vinegar

Combine the raspberry syrup and the vinegar in a small bowl. Gradually add the olive oil, whisking until the mixture

2 tablespoons extra virgin
olive oil

Salt and freshly ground black
pepper

is emulsified. Then add salt and pepper to taste. The vinai-grette will keep in an airtight container in the refrigerator for up to 1 week.

Trout Point Asparagus Vinaigrette

6 to 8 fresh asparagus spears

Salt and freshly ground black
pepper

¼ cup cider vinegar

¾ cup equal blend of olive
and canola oils

3 tablespoons unsalted butter

This unusual dressing works as stupendously with grilled fish fillets or other seafood as it does with salads.

1. Fill a mixing bowl halfway with ice and cold water, and set it aside.

2. Bring a small pot of salted water to a boil. Cut the tips off the asparagus, and set the spears aside. Blanch the tips in the boiling water until just tender, 1 minute. Immediately drain the tips and immerse them in the ice water bath to stop the cooking. When they are thoroughly cooled, chop the tips into very small pieces and set them aside.

3. Bring 1 cup water to a boil in a saucepan. Add the reserved asparagus spears and simmer until very soft but not falling apart, 10 to 12 minutes. Strain, discarding the spears and re-serving the cooking water. Return the cooking water to the saucepan and simmer until re-duced to about ¼ cup, 20 minutes. Season the reduction with salt and pepper.

4. Combine the reduction and half of the chopped asparagus tips in a mini food processor or blender, and puree.

5. In a small bowl, combine the puree with the vinegar. Add more salt and pepper if needed. Gradually add the oil blend, whisking constantly to form an emulsion. Set the dressing aside until ready to use.

6. Just before you serve the dressing, melt the butter gently over low heat. Whisk the melted butter into the vinaigrette, and stir in the remaining chopped asparagus tips. The vinaigrette will keep in an airtight container in the refrigerator for up to 4 days.

Creamy Herb Dressing

2 tablespoons good-quality
Asian fish sauce (such as
Three Crabs brand, see
page 61)

2 tablespoons rice wine
vinegar

1 garlic clove, minced

1 teaspoon dried thyme
or oregano leaves, or
1 tablespoon fresh, chopped

2 tablespoons extra virgin
olive oil

6 tablespoons heavy cream

½ teaspoon freshly ground
black pepper, optional

Although the ingredients look like a bizarre East-West fusion, this dressing packs vital flavors that bring out the taste of fresh romaine, arugula, and chicory. It has become our house standard.

Mix the fish sauce and vinegar together in a small bowl. Add the garlic and thyme, and stir. Slowly add the olive oil, whisking until the mixture is emulsified. Just before serving, whisk in the cream and add the optional black pepper. The dressing will keep in an airtight container in the refrigerator for up 4 days.

Maple Lemon Cream

4 tablespoons (½ stick)
unsalted butter, melted

6 tablespoons pure maple
syrup

3 tablespoons fresh lemon
juice

3 tablespoons heavy cream

The sweetness of the maple syrup and the tartness of the lemon juice fuse harmoniously to dress hearty green or mesclun salads.

Combine all the ingredients in a small bowl and whisk thoroughly. The dressing will keep in an airtight container in the refrigerator for up to 4 days.

Sugarcane Vinaigrette

¼ cup cane vinegar

Juice of ½ lime

Salt and freshly ground black
   pepper

1 tablespoon Asian fish sauce
   (see page 61)

1 teaspoon sugar

1 teaspoon minced garlic

½ cup extra virgin olive oil

A salad dressing with a hint of the Louisiana cane fields. This Cajun favorite is great with a wide range of salad greens.

Combine all the ingredients except the olive oil in a small bowl, and whisk to blend. Gradually add the olive oil, whisking constantly to form an emulsion. The vinaigrette will keep in an airtight container in the refrigerator for up to 1 week.

Blueberry Honey Vinaigrette

6 tablespoons rice wine
   vinegar

3 tablespoons blueberry honey

¼ cup pureed fresh or frozen
   blueberries

2 pinches salt

6 tablespoons olive oil

Blueberry bushes surround the Lodge, and each season we pick enough for desserts, pancakes, and just about anything else you can imagine, including this dressing.

Combine all the ingredients except the olive oil in a small bowl, and whisk to blend. Gradually add the olive oil, whisking constantly to form an emulsion. The vinaigrette will keep in an airtight container in the refrigerator for up to 4 days.

Chapter five

Entrées

In this fishery, we take also some dog sharks (chiens de mer) the skins of which the carpenters painstakingly guard to polish their joinery wood. Some hake (merlus) that are better than the cod, and sometimes Sea Bass: such diversity enhances our contentment. Those that do not tend towards cod nor towards fowl pass the time collecting the hearts, tripe, and the most delicate interior parts of the cod, which they make into a hash with lard, spices, and the flesh of the cod, producing sausages (cervelats) as good as those made in Paris. And in eating, it is bon apetit.

—Marc Lescarbot, *Histoire de la Nouvelle-France,* 1609

The Tusket River basin hosts an exceptional diversity of fish life. Some fish, including salmon, brook trout, gaspereau, shad, smelt, eel, and the rare Acadian whitefish, migrate toward the rivers, swimming upstream toward Trout Point. Local estuaries and the province's second-largest saltwater lake, Eel Lake, provide habitat for frost fish, striped bass, and succulent South Nova Scotia oysters. We often bring our cooking classes to Eel Lake to see the oysters and their plentiful cousins, the mussels, growing in nature. Clams, sea beans, and mussels thrive on the mudflats created by the receding eighteen-foot tides. Rocky seafloors shelter an abundance of lobster, scallops, crabs, and mussels. Schools of mackerel and herring abound to attract tuna, bluefish, and "dog fish" sharks like those described by Lescarbot in 1609. Groundfish species sought after by local fishermen include cod, monkfish, pollock, haddock, halibut, hake, and flounder.

At Trout Point Lodge, we call upon these culinary riches for simple entrées after three preceding courses at dinner and two at lunch. Creole dishes suit this way of serving, for they brim with diverse layers of flavor and make beautiful, singular presentations. In the Creole tradition inherited from our Louisiana roots, soups also often sneak their way into the entrée course, usually accompanied by rice. Gumbo is perhaps the most obvious example: a hearty, roux-based soup with layers of flavor and seasoning, it is completed with a panoply of fresh seafood. Other dishes that belong in this category include the classic Creole sauce matched with fresh shrimp or scallops, Fish and Mussel Bisque, and the elusive courtbouillon, which bears little resemblance to its French ancestor but truly captures the essence of Creole cooking. Jambalaya is of course the Creole world's paella.

We often grill the seafood we serve for lunch or dinner: the marvelous tuna found in Nova Scotia waters, swordfish, shark, squid, monkfish, trout, salmon, scallops, or sea trout. In Atlantic Canada, one needs little more than freshly caught seafood, fruity olive oil, and some sea salt to create an extraordinary meal.

At other times, more elegant (but still simple) preparations—almandine, *en papillote*—are on the menu. In this chapter, as throughout the book, we present some purely vegetarian recipes first, followed by seafood dishes, reflecting the food we serve at Trout Point Lodge.

Orecchiette with Spicy Chard Sauce

2 tablespoons extra virgin
   olive oil

4 dried red chiles, such as
   pepperoncino or cayenne

2 garlic cloves, chopped

1 ounce Marconi almonds,
   blanched, slivered almonds,
   or pine nuts

1 tablespoon Asian fish sauce
   (see page 61)

½ white onion, chopped

8 ounces dried orecchiette
   pasta

12 ounces fresh chard, leaves
   finely chopped, stems
   reserved for another use

¼ cup grated Parmigiano-
   Reggiano cheese

This method of cooking chard brings out its full, mineral-sweet flavors. (Save the chard stems for the Swiss Chard and Chestnut Gratinée on page 112.) We like this ear-shaped pasta because it holds bits of the sauce so well, enhancing the taste of this fantastic summer luncheon dish, but you can substitute another short, chunky type. If you cannot find Marconi almonds—a Spanish variety that is blanched, fried, and salted, and has a distinctive taste and texture—substitute blanched, slivered almonds or pine nuts.

1. Bring a large saucepan of salted water to a boil.

2. While the water is heating, heat the olive oil in a medium skillet over medium heat. Add the chiles and garlic, and sauté until the garlic begins to turn golden, about 7 minutes. Add the almonds and continue cooking until the garlic has caramelized, 8 to 10 minutes.

3. Lower the heat slightly and add the fish sauce and onion. Cook until the onion is transparent, about 8 minutes.

4. Meanwhile, add the pasta to the boiling water and cook until al dente, about 15 to 20 minutes, depending on the pasta. Drain in a colander.

5. Add the chopped chard to the sauce and cook until it has wilted and most of the liquid has evaporated, about 7 minutes.

6. In a large serving bowl, combine the pasta with the chard sauce. Top with the grated cheese, and serve immediately.

Creole-Style Lobster Mushrooms Etouffée

¼ cup canola or safflower oil

¼ cup unbleached all-purpose flour

2 white onions, diced

3 green bell peppers, chopped

4 celery stalks, diced

2 garlic cloves, finely diced

2 bay leaves

3 tomatoes, chopped and pureed in a blender or food processor

½ teaspoon cayenne pepper, or more to taste

½ teaspoon dried thyme leaves

¼ teaspoon dried oregano

¼ teaspoon freshly ground black pepper

Salt

8 ounces large lobster mushrooms, cut evenly into large pieces

1 tablespoon Asian fish sauce (see page 61)

6 cups cooked white rice

Etouffée means "smothered" in French. Louisiana Creoles and Cajuns make traditional étouffée dishes with crawfish, shrimp, or chicken. We have been using mushrooms for étouffée for years, and have discovered that one of our wild favorites, the colorful "lobster mushroom," works perfectly in this dish. You can't beat lobster mushrooms for a vegetarian étouffée, but you can substitute other meaty species, such as portobellos, if you can't find their rarer cousin.

For this Creole étouffée, we first make a dark roux, cooking flour in oil until it has an unforgettably fragrant, nutty aroma and a very dark brown color. You can make the sauce ahead of time and then sauté the mushrooms separately with a little butter, garlic, and/or onions; mix the warmed sauce with the mushrooms, and serve.

1. Heat the oil in a large, heavy saucepan over medium heat. Add the flour and cook, stirring, until the mixture is dark brown, 10 to 15 minutes.

2. Add the onions, bell peppers, celery, and garlic. Sauté the vegetables until they are soft and the onions are translucent, about 8 minutes.

3. Stir in the bay leaves and the tomato puree. Cook the sauce until it thickens, about 15 minutes.

4. Stir in the cayenne, thyme, oregano, black pepper, and salt to taste. Add the lobster mushrooms and cook for another 5 minutes. Add the fish sauce and cook for an additional 5 minutes. Remove the bay leaves and serve immediately over hot rice.

Mushroom-Oyster-Artichoke Sauce
with Penne

1 cup unbleached all-purpose
  flour

1 teaspoon salt

1½ teaspoons freshly ground
  black pepper

8 ounces fresh oysters

1 cup extra virgin olive oil

6 small artichokes

6 large fresh shiitake
  mushrooms, sliced

10 large fresh white button
  or cremini mushrooms,
  sliced

1 tablespoon herbes de
  Provence

1 cup medium-dry white wine,
  such as a white Bordeaux

Sea salt

1 pound good-quality dried
  penne

¼ cup grated Parmigiano-
  Reggiano cheese

2 tablespoons Asian fish sauce
  (see page 61) or tamari
  sauce

Woodsy mushrooms, delicious sweet oysters, and the refreshing nutty flavor and slight bitterness of artichokes make for an enchanting Creole alchemy that satisfies every palate.

1. Mix together the flour, 1 teaspoon salt, and 1 teaspoon pepper. Dredge the oysters in this mixture. Heat ¼ cup of the oil in a large skillet over medium-high heat. Fry the oysters until they are golden brown, about 3 minutes. Remove them from the pan and drain on paper towels. Refrigerate until ready to use.

2. Trim off all but the tender inner leaves of the artichokes, and trim about ½ inch off the tops. Cut the artichokes in half.

3. Heat ½ cup of the olive oil in a large skillet over medium-high heat. Add the artichoke halves and sauté until they begin to brown, 8 to 10 minutes on each side. Add 3 tablespoons water, cover, and steam over medium-low heat until they are tender, about 5 minutes. Set them aside.

4. Heat the remaining ¼ cup olive oil in a large saucepan over medium heat. Add the sliced mushrooms and sauté until tender, about 5 minutes.

5. Add the herbes de Provence, white wine, and sea salt to taste. Simmer until the liquid is reduced by half, about 8 minutes.

6. Meanwhile, bring a large pot of salted water to a boil. Add the penne and cook until *almost* al dente, about 12 minutes. Drain, and add the penne to the sauce.

7. Cook over low heat until the penne is done, about 5 more minutes. Then add the cheese, fish sauce, remaining ½ teaspoon of pepper, and the oysters. Mix thoroughly, taste for seasoning, and serve.

Vegetable Shepherd's Pie

SERVES 4

3 cups dried bread crumbs

2 cups grated sharp Cheddar
  or Gruyère cheese

¼ cup olive oil

1 tablespoon dried thyme
  leaves

1 medium eggplant

2 medium zucchini

3 large yellow squash

2 teaspoons salt

2 cups Creole Red Beans
  (page 111), without rice

6 cups mashed potatoes
  (recipe follows)

Fresh summer vegetables make this traditional Creole dish come alive with flavor. It's worth making fresh mashed potatoes just for the occasion—although of course it's a great way to use leftovers.

1. Preheat the oven to 350° F.

2. Line the sides and bottom of a square baking pan or glass casserole with aluminum foil, and grease it liberally with butter or oil.

3. In a small mixing bowl, blend together the bread crumbs and cheese. Set it aside.

4. In another small bowl, mix together the olive oil and thyme.

5. Cut the eggplant, zucchini, and yellow squash into ¼-inch slices. Sprinkle the salt over the slices. Coat the slices in the olive oil mixture, and arrange them in a single layer in a large baking pan. Roast in the oven, turning once, until just tender, about 8 minutes.

6. Assemble the dish: Arrange the eggplant in a single layer in the prepared baking dish, cutting the slices as necessary to fit. Top the eggplant with a sprinkling of the bread crumb mixture. Next, create a layer of the zucchini slices and top it with a sprinkling of the bread crumb mixture. Follow with a layer of yellow squash slices and the last of the bread crumb mixture. Then spread the Creole Red Beans over the top. Cover with the mashed potatoes.

7. Cover the baking dish tightly with aluminum foil, and bake for 1 hour.

8. Remove the dish from the oven and remove the foil. Allow the pie to cool for about 15 minutes, and then cut it into individual servings.

Mashed Potatoes

2 tablespoons salt, plus more
to taste

6 Idaho or Yukon Gold
potatoes

1 cup heavy cream, warmed

8 tablespoons (1 stick)
unsalted butter, softened

Freshly ground black pepper

1. Bring a large pot of water to a boil, and add 2 tablespoons salt. While the water is heating, peel the potatoes.

2. Add the potatoes to the boiling water and cook until thoroughly tender, 15 to 20 minutes.

3. Drain the potatoes and let them cool in a large mixing bowl for about 5 minutes. Then add the cream and butter, and mash thoroughly. Season with salt and pepper to taste, and serve.

Creole Stuffed Bell Peppers

SERVES 4

5 tablespoons extra virgin
   olive oil

3 white onions, sliced

3 celery stalks, chopped

2 carrots, finely chopped

3 garlic cloves, chopped

1 teaspoon chopped fresh
   thyme

1 teaspoon chopped fresh
   oregano

½ teaspoon cayenne pepper

½ cup coarsely chopped fresh
   white button mushrooms

½ cup sliced fresh shiitake
   mushrooms

6 cups long-grain white rice

¾ cup Mushroom Stock
   (page 46) or Vegetable Stock
   (page 55)

1 tablespoon sea salt

½ teaspoon freshly ground
   black pepper

4 large green bell peppers

This vegetarian version of a great Louisiana comfort food uses mushrooms and fresh herbs for substantial flavor.

1. Preheat the oven to 400° F.

2. Heat the olive oil in a large sauté pan or saucepan over medium heat. Add the onions, celery, and carrots, and cook until the vegetables are soft and the onions are translucent, 7 minutes.

3. Add the garlic, thyme, oregano, and cayenne, and sauté briefly, until fragrant. Add the button and shiitake mushrooms and cook, stirring frequently, for 2 minutes.

4. Add the rice to the pan, mixing it thoroughly with the other ingredients, and cook for another 2 minutes.

5. Add the stock, salt, and pepper. Bring to a boil, reduce the heat, and simmer for 5 minutes.

6. Remove the pan from the heat, and allow the mixture to cool. Cut the tops off the peppers, and remove the seeds and membranes. Fill the peppers evenly with the rice stuffing, and bake until they are tender, about 35 minutes. Serve.

Creole Stuffed Eggplants

2 large or 4 medium eggplants

1 cup extra virgin olive oil

1 tablespoon canola or olive oil

1 tablespoon unbleached
all-purpose flour

1 medium onion, chopped

1 small fresh hot chile, such
as Serrano, chopped

1½ tablespoons chopped fresh
lovage

3 garlic cloves, chopped

1 medium tomato, chopped

1 teaspoon hot pepper sauce,
such as Tabasco or Crystal

1 tablespoon Worcestershire
sauce

2 tablespoons Asian fish sauce
(see page 61)

1 teaspoon salt

Freshly ground black pepper

¾ cup dried bread crumbs

6 tablespoons grated
Parmigiano-Reggiano cheese

1 egg white

Italian immigrants to Louisiana found a welcoming climate for growing *melanzane*, and they soon developed a distinctive cuisine known as Creole Italian. Many of the Louisiana Italians, who hailed mostly from Sicily, opened restaurants and food stores in New Orleans— Central Grocery in the French Quarter is one example. If you like, add ¼ cup mashed tofu for a shot of protein.

1. Preheat the oven to 400° F.

2. Cut the eggplants in half and hollow out the centers, leaving a ½-inch-thick shell. Coarsely chop the scooped-out pulp and set aside. Rub the halved shells, inside and out, with ½ cup of the olive oil, and place them in a baking dish.

3. Bake the eggplant shells until just soft, about 15 minutes. Set them aside. Lower the oven temperature to 325°.

4. Heat the tablespoon of oil in a large, heavy saucepan over medium heat. Add the flour and cook, stirring, until peanut butter–colored, about 10 minutes. Add one-fourth of the chopped onion, the chile pepper, and the lovage, and sauté for about 2 minutes. Add the garlic, the remaining ½ cup of olive oil, and the remaining chopped onion. Cook until the onion is soft, about 7 minutes.

5. Lower the heat to medium and add the tomato, hot sauce, Worcestershire sauce, fish sauce, salt, black pepper, and about 2 tablespoons water—enough to make a thick sauce-like consistency. Cook for 2 minutes. Add the reserved eggplant pulp, and cook until all the ingredients have softened, about 5 minutes.

6. Add ½ cup of the bread crumbs and 3 tablespoons of the cheese. Take the pan off the heat.

7. Beat the egg white lightly in a bowl, and combine it thoroughly with the stuffing mixture. Stuff the eggplant halves, and dust the tops with the remaining bread crumbs and the remaining cheese.

8. Bake until the cheese and bread crumbs have browned, 15 to 20 minutes. Serve immediately.

Creole Red Beans and Rice

1 pound dried red kidney
   beans

3 tablespoons extra virgin
   olive oil

2 ounces sliced smoked
   salmon, optional

3 celery stalks, finely chopped

1 large green bell pepper,
   finely chopped

3 garlic cloves, finely chopped

1 medium onion, finely
   chopped

1 teaspoon dried thyme leaves

2 teaspoons hot pepper sauce,
   such as Tabasco or Crystal

1 teaspoon salt

2 bay leaves

Freshly ground black pepper

2 cups long-grain white rice

2 tablespoon Asian fish sauce
   (see page 61), optional

This Louisiana classic is served traditionally every Monday in New Orleans, and now it is in Nova Scotia too. We always serve white rice with red beans.

1. Pick through the beans, removing any stones or debris, and then rinse them under cold running water. Place them in a bowl, add cold water to cover, and let them soak overnight.

2. Heat the olive oil in a stockpot or Dutch oven over medium heat. Add the smoked salmon, if using, and sauté until fragrant, about 7 minutes.

3. Add the celery and sauté until slightly tender, about 2 minutes. Add the bell pepper and cook for 1 minute. Then add the garlic and onion, and cook until the onion is translucent and all the ingredients are tender, about 8 minutes.

4. Drain the beans and add them to the pot. Add enough water to cover, approximately 6 cups. Turn the heat to high and add the thyme, hot sauce, salt, bay leaves, and black pepper. Cook for 3 to 4 minutes.

5. Reduce the heat to low, cover, and simmer until the beans are tender, about 1½ hours.

6. About 20 minutes before the beans are done, prepare the rice according to the package.

7. Add the fish sauce to the beans. Taste the beans for seasoning, and serve over the hot rice.

Swiss Chard and Chestnut Gratinée

3 cups Swiss chard stalks
chopped into 1-inch pieces

For the blanc

Juice of 1 lemon plus
6 tablespoons, or
11 tablespoons white vinegar

¼ cup unbleached all-purpose
flour

1 tablespoon salt

20 chestnuts, roasted, shelled,
and roughly chopped, or
¾ cup blanched, coarsely
chopped almonds

4 tablespoons extra virgin
olive oil

1 medium sweet onion, such
as Vidalia, chopped

1 medium leek (white and
light green parts), well
rinsed and cut into ½-inch
pieces

4 garlic cloves, diced

2 medium tomatoes, coarsely
chopped

**SERVES 4 AS AN ENTREE,
6 AS AN APPETIZER OR SIDE DISH**

Chard thrives in Trout Point's summer climate, growing into meaty, delicious stalks with brilliant green leaves. This recipe uses only the stalk, allowing you to utilize the leaves in another tantalizing recipe, such as Orecchiette with Spicy Chard Sauce (page 103). We often make this gratinée as an appetizer, using individual ramekins rather than a larger casserole dish. You can also decide whether or not to add the shellfish. Red chard will work as well as white; since it won't discolor like white chard, it eliminates the need for a *blanc*. Your favorite nut can be substituted for the chestnuts in a pinch, but we think chestnuts combine best with the hearty chard stalks.

1. Preheat the oven to 400° F.

2. *If you are using red Swiss chard,* remove the leaves and reserve them for another use. Chop the stems into 1-inch pieces. You should have 3 cups. Bring a large pot of water to a boil, and add the chard.

   If you are using white Swiss chard, first fill a large bowl halfway with cold water and add the juice of 1 lemon or 5 tablespoons of the vinegar. Then remove the Swiss chard leaves and reserve them for another use. Chop the stems into 1-inch pieces; you should have 3 cups. Put the chopped stems in the vinegar water. Now prepare a *blanc*: Set out a large pot to use for cooking the chard. Put the flour in a fine-mesh strainer, set the strainer over the pot,

Salt and freshly ground black
  pepper
1 teaspoon dried oregano
¾ cup dried bread crumbs,
  preferably homemade
  from toasted whole-grain
  bread
1 pound fresh clams, oysters,
  mussels, or a combination,
  steamed open and shucked,
  optional
1 cup crumbled or grated
  cheese: a mixture of fresh
  goat cheese and 1 or 2 firm,
  aged cheeses like
  Manchego, Cantal, or
  Gruyère

and pour 4 quarts cold water through the strainer into the pot. Mix the flour well with the water. Stir in the remaining 6 tablespoons of lemon juice (or remaining vinegar) and the salt. Drain the chard, add it to the *blanc,* and bring to a boil over high heat.

3. Reduce the heat to a simmer and add the chestnuts. Simmer until the chard stalks are just tender, about 10 minutes. Drain and separate the chestnuts from the chard stalks. Coarsely chop the chestnuts. Set both aside.

4. Heat 2 tablespoons of the olive oil in a skillet over medium heat. Add the onion, leek, and garlic, and sauté until fragrant, 7 to 8 minutes.

5. Add the tomatoes, salt and pepper to taste, and the oregano. Sauté just until the tomatoes are soft (do not overcook), about 6 minutes. Remove from the heat and set aside.

6. Heat a heavy-bottom skillet over medium heat. Heat the bread crumbs in the pan to crisp them, about 3 minutes.

7. Pour the remaining 2 tablespoons olive oil evenly over the bread crumbs. Add the chopped chestnuts and sauté until they are very crisp, about 5 minutes.

8. Combine the tomato mixture and the chard stalks in a shallow baking dish. (If you are using individual ramekins, fill each one about halfway.) Add the optional shellfish. Arrange the bread crumbs–chestnut mixture over the vegetables. Cover evenly with the cheese, and bake until the cheese turns golden brown, about 20 minutes. Cool for 5 minutes before serving.

Preparing a *Blanc* for Vegetables

Some vegetables, like white Swiss chard, artichokes, salsify, and celery root, tend to discolor when they are cooked. Using a *blanc* is a great technique for preventing this.

First, before chopping or peeling the vegetable, fill a bowl halfway with cold water to which you have added the juice of 1 lemon or 5 tablespoons vinegar. As soon as you have prepared the vegetable, place it in this acidulated water.

Now prepare the *blanc:* For 4 quarts of water, you will need ¼ cup unbleached all-purpose flour, 1 tablespoon salt, and 6 tablespoons lemon juice. Put the flour in a fine-mesh strainer, and set the strainer over the pot in which you will cook the vegetables. Pour the cold water through the strainer into the pot. Thoroughly mix the flour with the cold water, creating a suspension of flour in the water. Stir in the lemon juice or vinegar and the salt. Drain the vegetable, add it to the *blanc,* and place the pot over high heat. Bring the water to a boil and cook the vegetable as directed in the recipe.

Monkfish with Garlic-Tomato Sauce

4 tomatoes

½ cup unbleached all-purpose
flour

½ teaspoon sea salt

½ teaspoon freshly ground
black pepper

Canola or peanut oil

1 large monkfish, boned and
cut into six 4- to 5-ounce
steaks

½ cup extra virgin olive oil

Three ½-inch-thick slices
day-old French bread

¼ cup blanched almonds,
toasted

4 plump garlic cloves

1 teaspoon rice wine vinegar

1 teaspoon salt

1 cup dry white wine

1 teaspoon chipotle pepper
powder or ground chipotle

1 tablespoon Asian fish sauce
(see page 61)

2 tablespoons sweet paprika

1 teaspoon hot paprika

In this recipe we pair the lively flavors and brilliant red color of the sauce—made by using traditional techniques found in both Andalusian Spanish and Mexican cuisine—with sweet, ivory-colored monkfish steaks. (Anyone who has made Mexican mole will feel right at home with this recipe.) The two-stage cooking process for the fish steaks ensures a pleasing variety of texture.

1. Spear a tomato on a long-handled fork and hold it over an open flame, rotating it, until the skin cracks and chars. Cut the tomato in half, remove the seeds, and place the halves in a medium mixing bowl. Repeat with the remaining tomatoes. Alternately the tomatoes can be placed on a baking sheet and roasted under a broiler, turning so that the skin on all sides cracks and chars. Set aside.

2. Stir the flour, sea salt, and pepper together in a wide, shallow bowl.

3. Pour canola oil into a medium, nonstick skillet to a depth of ¼ inch, and place it over medium heat.

4. Coat the monkfish steaks in the flour mixture and sauté them in the hot oil for about 5 minutes on each side, or until the flour coating begins to brown. Do not cook the steaks all the way; they will finish cooking in the sauce. Put the steaks aside. (This step may done up to 1 hour in advance.)

5. Heat ¼ cup of the olive oil in a medium nonstick skillet over medium heat and fry the bread, turning it once, until both sides are golden brown and crisp, 2 to 3 minutes per side. Set the toast aside and reserve the skillet.

6. Using a large mortar and pestle, smash together the toasted almonds, garlic, vinegar, and the teaspoon of salt. You may also use a food processor for this step.

7. Crush the reserved tomatoes with your fingers to create a sauce-like consistency. Be sure to leave some charred skin.

8. Add the toasted bread and about ¼ cup of the tomatoes to the ingredients in the mortar and pound together to form a thick paste, leaving some larger pieces of almond for texture.

9. Empty the contents of the mortar into the bowl with the remaining tomatoes. Add the white wine, chipotle powder, fish sauce, and paprikas, and blend everything together. Heat the remaining ¼ cup of olive oil in the skillet used to cook the bread. Add the tomato-wine mixture and cook until fragrant, about 2 minutes.

10. Add the monkfish steaks to the sauce, lower the heat, cover the skillet, and cook until the steaks are very tender but not breaking apart, about 15 minutes. Do not cover the steaks with the sauce or turn them, as you want to preserve the beautiful ivory color of the fish.

11. Place each steak on a warmed plate, surround it with sauce, and serve immediately.

Salmon Baked in Salt with Fresh Dill

SERVES 6

1 extremely fresh 4-pound whole salmon, trout, or sea trout, gutted, bones and head retained

1 cup coarsely chopped fresh dill leaves and stems, plus whole sprigs for garnish

6 pounds additive-free coarse salt

We demonstrate this technique to all of our classes at the Nova Scotia Seafood Cooking School, which is held at the Lodge every summer and fall. Salt crusting appears difficult but is actually an easy technique for cooking any of the members of the salmon family—including sea trout, freshwater trout, salmon, and arctic char—and certainly makes for an elegant presentation. Here we use fresh dill to stuff the body cavity, but you can use any fresh aromatic herb—sage, for example. You can reuse the salt to bake fish another time. If you have *poissonnière* or another suitable container, you can get away with using less salt. Simply ensure there is an even layer—at least ½ inch thick—all the way around the fish.

1. Preheat the oven to 385° F.

2. Stuff the cavity of the fish with the chopped dill. Fill a baking dish or *poissonnière* with a ½-inch-deep layer of salt. Place the fish, top fins up, on the salt. Pour the remaining salt over the fish until you have a layer at least ½ inch thick around the fish's body without covering the head or the tail fin. If you want, mold aluminum foil to hold the salt against the fish.

3. Bake for 45 minutes, or about 10 minutes per pound plus an extra 5 minutes.

4. To serve, remove the salt by breaking off the large pieces that have crusted near the fish's body. With the fish lying on its side and using a flexible knife, cut out individual fillets with vertical cuts that go almost all the way to the bone. Remove these fillets onto plates using a spatula or wide knife; they should pull away easily from the spine. Turn the fish over and repeat, removing more fillets from the other side. Or, if you prefer, use a fork to remove smaller pieces rather than larger fillets, piling the pieces onto plates. Garnish with fresh dill sprigs.

Salmon Cakes

1 medium new potato

2 pounds cooked salmon (leftovers from the salt-baked salmon on page 117 work perfectly)

½ cup chopped green bell pepper

1 small onion, chopped

⅔ cup grated Parmigiano-Reggiano cheese

Grated zest of 1½ lemons

¼ cup chopped celery

½ cup dried bread crumbs

Salt and freshly ground black pepper

SERVES 6 AS AN ENTREE, 10 AS AN APPETIZER

With Nova Scotia as home to the best salmon in the world, we get rave reviews from guests for these cakes that meld fresh Acadian salmon and exhilarating Cajun seasonings. You may want to make smaller-size cakes for appetizer portions.

1. Bring a small saucepan of water to a boil, add the potato, and boil until it has cooked through, 15 minutes. Drain the potato and place it in a mixing bowl.

2. Break the cooked salmon into small pieces.

3. Coarsely mash the potato. Add the bell pepper, onion, cheese, lemon zest, celery, and salmon, and combine well. Add 3 tablespoons of the bread crumbs. Season with salt and pepper to taste.

¼ cup egg whites, lightly
   beaten
¼ cup extra virgin olive oil
Salmon Cake Sauce (recipe
   follows)

4. Place the remaining bread crumbs on one plate, and the egg whites on another.

5. Using your hands, form the salmon mixture into cakes about the size of hamburger patties. Dip each cake into the egg whites and then coat it with bread crumbs.

6. Heat the olive oil in a large nonstick skillet over medium-high heat. Sauté the salmon cakes, flipping them once, until the exterior has browned, 10 minutes. Serve immediately, with the sauce alongside.

Salmon Cake Sauce

SERVES 6

3 tablespoons mayonnaise

2 tablespoons extra virgin
olive oil

1 tablespoon prepared
horseradish, drained

2 tablespoon onion relish

Mix all the ingredients thoroughly in a small bowl. Spoon over the salmon cakes or serve alongside.

Marinated Swordfish Kebabs

SERVES 6

2¼ pounds fresh swordfish,
cut into 1-inch-thick steaks

Juice of 2 lemons

½ cup extra virgin olive oil,
plus extra for grilling

2 garlic cloves, minced

Salt and freshly ground black
pepper

8 fresh bay leaves, or
substitute dried

2 onions, cut into thick
slices

2 tomatoes, cut into thick
wedges

2 green or red bell peppers,
cut into 1-inch squares

6 lemon or lime leaves,
cut in half

Grilling swordfish with bay and citrus leaves infuses this very simple summertime dish with a delicious blend of savory flavors. You can substitute shark or halibut for the swordfish if you desire.

1. If using wooden skewers, soak them in warm water for 30 minutes.

2. Cut the swordfish steaks into 1-inch square chunks.

3. In a large glass or ceramic bowl, mix together the lemon juice, olive oil, garlic, and salt and pepper to taste. Coarsely chop 2 of the bay leaves, and add them.

4. Add the swordfish to this marinade, and stir well. Cover and allow the fish to marinate for at least 2 hours at room temperature.

5. Cut the remaining 6 bay leaves in half.

6. Heat an outdoor grill or an indoor grill pan until it is very hot.

7. Coat the onion pieces with olive oil and grill them until they soften and begin to caramelize, about 10 minutes.

8. Using wooden or metal skewers, prepare kebobs, alternating tomatoes, onions, and bell peppers with the swordfish, lemon leaves, and bay leaves. Always place a lemon or bay leaf directly next to a piece of swordfish.

9. Grill for about 15 minutes, turning the skewers every 4 or 5 minutes, until the pieces of swordfish are thoroughly cooked and slightly charred on the outside. The vegetables should be cooked but still somewhat firm. Remove the skewers and serve hot.

Scallops with Ginger-Scallion Sauce

SERVES 4

12 ounces fresh scallops,
   as large as possible
5 quarter-size rounds of
   peeled ginger, smashed with
   the side of a knife
5 scallions (white part only),
   cut into 1-inch pieces
3 tablespoons unsalted butter
¼ cup dry vermouth
Salt and white pepper
¼ cup heavy cream

The huge, juicy scallops from the waters off southwestern Nova Scotia deserve their fame, and we serve them religiously every summer when the boat captain in the nearby port of Yarmouth calls for us to come collect our order. In many of today's supermarkets, scallops come either "dry" or artificially injected with water. The best scallops, like those we see in Nova Scotia, are naturally plump, pearly white or sometimes pinkish, and always sweet-smelling and fresh. The ginger-scallion sauce lends luscious depth to the grilled scallop's sweetness. This effortless recipe makes a great lunch entrée, especially when it is preceded by the Swiss Chard and Chestnut Gratinée (page 112) as an appetizer.

1. Clean the scallops and set them aside.

2. Combine the ginger and scallions in a food processor, and finely chop.

3. Melt the butter in a small saucepan over low heat. Add the ginger mixture and cook until fragrant, about 1 minute. Add half of the vermouth, and salt and white pepper to taste. Cook

until the mixture reduces slightly, about 8 minutes. Add the remaining vermouth and the cream. Keep the sauce warm over very low heat while you prepare the scallops.

4. Heat a nonstick skillet or grill pan over high heat. Add the scallops and cook just until they start to brown, about 3 minutes on each side. Do not overcook, or the scallops will become tough and will lose their sweetness.

5. Serve immediately, topped with the ginger-scallion sauce.

Smoked Salmon Spaghetti alla Carbonara

SERVES 4

4 large eggs

Sea salt

1 pound dried spaghetti

¼ cup extra virgin olive oil

4 ounces Salmon Bacon
    (page 212) or smoked
    salmon, thinly sliced

1 tablespoon freshly ground
    black pepper

½ cup grated Parmigiano-
    Reggiano cheese

½ cup grated aged Canadian
    white Cheddar cheese

Our Nova Scotia version of this famous pasta dish adds smoked salmon and Canadian white Cheddar. As with all true carbonara dishes, the secret lies in having the pan at the correct temperature so the eggs coat the spaghetti in this delicious sauce, which should have a satiny, not a scrambled-egg, texture.

1. Whisk the eggs with a pinch of salt in a small mixing bowl. Set it aside.

2. Bring a large pot of water to a boil and add 2 tablespoons sea salt. Add the spaghetti and cook until al dente, 10 to 18 minutes. Drain the spaghetti thoroughly in a colander.

3. While the pasta is cooking, heat the olive oil in a large skillet over medium heat. Add the Salmon Bacon and sauté until it is fragrant and crisp, about 5 minutes.

4. Reduce the heat to medium-low and add the drained pasta to the skillet. Toss the pasta to thoroughly coat it with the oil. Remove the skillet from the heat and immediately add the eggs, tossing the pasta rapidly to coat it with the eggs. (You want to avoid cooking the eggs, so you must work quickly and keep the mixture moving.) Add the pepper and half of each of the cheeses. Toss thoroughly and serve, with the remaining grated cheeses on top.

Saffron Seafood Gnocchi

10 medium shrimp, peeled
and deveined, shells and
heads reserved

1 tablespoon Asian fish sauce
(see page 61)

1 teaspoon salt

3 pinches saffron threads

¼ cup plus 2 tablespoons
extra virgin olive oil

5 large garlic cloves, finely
chopped

1 pound gnocchi, preferably
fresh, or defrosted frozen

8 ounces clam strips in their
liquor, or 8 ounces clams,
sliced

2 Roma (plum) tomatoes,
coarsely chopped and lightly
salted

25 salted pistachios, shelled

8 large fresh scallops

1 tablespoon unbleached
all-purpose flour

Sea salt

¼ cup plus 2 tablespoons
grated Parmigiano-Reggiano
cheese

1. Put the shrimp shells and heads in a saucepan, and add the fish sauce and salt. Add 1 cup water and bring to a boil. Simmer until the liquid has reduced by one-fourth, about 10 minutes.

2. Reduce the heat, add the saffron, and simmer briefly, just until the liquid turns yellow. Remove the pan from the heat, strain the shrimp stock, and set it aside.

3. Heat ¼ cup of the olive oil in a large skillet over medium heat. Add the garlic and sauté just until fragrant, 2 minutes. Remove the skillet from the heat. (You may prepare the recipe to this point up to 3 hours in advance.)

4. Bring a large pot of salted water to a boil, add the gnocchi, and cook until not quite al dente, 12 minutes. Drain the gnocchi and set aside.

5. Add ½ cup of the shrimp stock to the garlic in the skillet, and place the skillet over medium heat. Cook until reduced by one-fourth, about 5 minutes. Then add the clam strips and their liquor, and cook for another 5 minutes.

6. Add the tomatoes and the pistachios, and cook until the tomatoes are very soft, 3 minutes. Add the shrimp and scallops. If the mixture seems dry, add more of the shrimp stock.

7. Stir in the flour. Cover, and cook over medium heat until the scallops are cooked, 3 minutes.

8. Add the remaining 2 tablespoons of olive oil and the gnocchi. Mix well, cover, and cook for another 1 to 2 minutes, or until the pasta is done and has incorporated some of the sauce. Taste for salt, top with the grated cheese, and serve.

Swordfish with Almond-Garlic Sauce

SERVES 6

Juice of 1 orange

¾ cup extra virgin olive oil, or more as needed

6 swordfish steaks, 6 ounces each and about ½ inch thick

6 large garlic cloves, crushed with the side of a knife

3 slices day-old baguette, 1¼ inches thick

¼ cup Marconi almonds, or whole, blanched almonds

¼ cup plus 2 tablespoons dry white wine, or more as needed

Salt

This recipe uses cooking techniques common to both Spain and Creole Latin America. The sauce lends texture and rich flavor to the grilled swordfish. You can substitute any other meaty fish, like tuna or shark. Use Marconi almonds if available. They're a Spanish variety that is blanched, then fried and salted, and has a distinctive taste and texture.

1. Combine the orange juice and ¼ plus 2 tablespoons of the olive oil in a shallow glass dish. Add the swordfish steaks, cover, and marinate for at least 1 hour, and up to 4 hours in the refrigerator.

2. Heat the remaining ¼ cup plus 2 tablespoons olive oil in a medium skillet over medium heat. Add the garlic cloves and sauté until they begin to brown, about 5 minutes. Add the bread slices and fry on both sides until golden, about 5 minutes. Add the almonds and fry for another 3 minutes.

3. Transfer the contents of the skillet, including the olive oil, to a mortar. Add the white wine and grind all the ingredients with a pestle to create a rough mixture, leaving large chunks of almonds. (You can use a food processor for this, but be careful not to make too fine a paste.) Add more wine or olive oil as needed, but do not wet the sauce too much; it should clump together. Season with salt to taste.

4. Heat a grill pan or a nonstick skillet over high heat.

5. Recoat the swordfish steaks with the marinade, and cook on each side for about 4 minutes, or until thoroughly cooked.

6. Top with the almond-garlic sauce, and serve.

Tuna Napoleon with Sweet Red Pepper Sauce

4 medium to large tomatoes, cut into ½-inch-thick slices

½ cup plus 2 tablespoons extra virgin olive oil, plus extra for the tomatoes

Salt

½ cup plus 2 tablespoons canola oil

¼ cup dried oregano, or ½ cup fresh oregano, chopped

4 medium eggplants, peeled and cut into sixteen ½-inch-thick slices

4 fresh tuna fillets, 1 inch thick, cut lengthwise in half

Freshly ground black pepper

20 fresh Thai basil leaves, or sweet basil leaves

8 thin slices Parmigiano-Reggiano cheese

¼ cup plus 2 tablespoons dry red wine

Sweet Red Pepper Sauce (recipe follows)

This is a great dish for late-summer parties. All of the ingredients can be prepared in advance and then assembled at the last minute.

1. Preheat the broiler.

2. Coat the tomato slices with olive oil, and sprinkle them with salt. Place them in a single layer on a baking sheet, and broil until they are thoroughly cooked but not falling apart, 5 minutes. Transfer the tomatoes to a plate and let them cool.

3. Stir the olive oil, canola oil, and oregano together in a bowl. Measure out ¼ cup of this mixture and set it aside.

4. Heat a large, heavy skillet over medium-high heat, and add about ¼ cup of the remaining oil mixture. When it is hot, add as many eggplant slices as will fit and sauté until they are thoroughly cooked and are beginning to expel the oil, 10 minutes. Transfer the slices to a plate. Heat more oil mixture and continue sautéing until all the slices are cooked. Let them cool on the plate.

5. Preheat the broiler or an indoor or outdoor grill. Coat the tuna slices liberally with the reserved ¼ cup oil mixture, and season them with salt and pepper to taste. Broil or grill the tuna steaks, turning them over once, until cooked to your liking, 6 to 10 minutes. They should be pink at the center—do not overcook them. Remove the tuna from the heat.

6. Preheat the oven to 300° F.

7. Assemble the napoleons on a rimmed baking sheet: Place an eggplant slice on the baking sheet and top it with a piece of tuna. Layer a tomato slice over the tuna, followed by several

basil leaves. Add another eggplant slice and then a slice of Parmigiano. Repeat, making 8 napoleons. Sprinkle the red wine over the napoleons, place the baking sheet in the oven, and bake until they are thoroughly warmed, 5 minutes.

8. Top each napoleon with 3 tablespoons of Sweet Red Pepper Sauce, and serve immediately.

Sweet Red Pepper Sauce

MAKES 2 CUPS

1¼ cup plus 2 tablespoons
  extra virgin olive oil, or more
  as needed
1 small onion, sliced
3 red bell peppers, cut into
  1-inch slices
1 plump garlic clove, cut in half
1 teaspoon herbes de Provence
Salt
½ teaspoon freshly ground
  black pepper
½ teaspoon sugar, optional

1. Heat 2 tablespoons of the olive oil in a small skillet over medium heat. Add the onion and sauté until caramelized, 8 to 10 minutes. Remove the skillet from the heat.

2. Heat an indoor grill pan over medium heat. Coat the red pepper slices in ¼ cup of olive oil, and place them on the pan. Grill until they are soft and the skin is charred, 10 to 14 minutes. Set the peppers aside to cool slightly, and then remove all or most of the charred skin, to your taste.

3. Combine the peppers, onion, garlic, herbes de Provence, salt to taste, black pepper, and optional sugar in a food processor or blender. Process, gradually adding the remaining cup of olive oil, until the mixture forms a thick sauce. Add more olive oil if the sauce is too thick or dry.

4. Serve hot. The sauce will keep for up to 5 days in the refrigerator.

Thai Basil

Thai basil has a pure, sweet licorice-like flavor without any herbaceous or grassy overtones, and is extremely flavorful. It is one of our favorite basils to use for garnishes, as a fresh herb, or for pesto. The leaves are green with a distinct purple cast. Thai basil can be found in Chinese grocery stores and can also be grown from seed.

Grilled Shark Steaks with Sage Butter Sauce

¼ cup extra virgin olive oil

Juice of 1 lemon

Freshly ground black pepper

¼ teaspoon cayenne pepper

¼ teaspoon garlic powder

¼ teaspoon dried thyme leaves

6 shark steaks, preferably
  mako, 6 to 8 ounces each
  and ¾ inch thick

8 tablespoons (1 stick)
  unsalted butter

2 tablespoons coarsely
  chopped fresh sage

Many of our guests taste shark for the first time at the Lodge, and we always marvel at the fact that so many people have avoided eating what is an excellent and usually inexpensive fish. Prepared correctly, shark is tender and will remind meat-lovers of their favorite sirloin. There is no better way to cook shark than simply grilling it after a brief marinade.

1. Combine the olive oil, lemon juice, black pepper, cayenne, garlic powder, and thyme in a baking dish. Add the shark steaks, cover and marinate for at least 2 hours in the refrigerator, flipping them after the first hour.

2. Heat an indoor grill pan over medium-high heat, or prepare an outdoor grill.

3. While the pan is heating, prepare the sage butter sauce: Melt the butter in a small saucepan over medium-low heat. Add the chopped sage leaves, stirring them in until fragrant. Keep the sauce warm over very low heat.

4. Remove the shark steaks from the marinade and put them on the heated grill pan. Pour any remaining marinade over the steaks. Grill for about 5 minutes on each side. (You can test for doneness with a knife, as you would a beef steak.)

5. Serve immediately, topping each steak with 1 to 2 tablespoons of the sage butter sauce.

Spicy Cornmeal-Crusted Scallops with Wild Sweet Fern Butter

4 pepperoncini or other small, flavorful dried red peppers, crushed

¼ cup unbleached all-purpose flour

½ cup yellow cornmeal

½ teaspoon dried thyme leaves

Salt and freshly ground black pepper

4 tablespoons (½ stick) unsalted butter

⅓ cup very coarsely chopped sweet fern or fresh sage leaves

1 pound large fresh scallops

5 tablespoons olive oil

SERVES 6

With just a few minutes of preparation time, this dish blends the flavors of New Orleans with North Atlantic scallops and the deep, woodsy taste of wild sweet fern (see page 72), a plant that grows around the Lodge. The scallops should be plump and moist to receive the coating of cornmeal and spices; if they aren't, soak them in milk for about 5 minutes before preparing them.

1. On a large plate, mix together the pepperoncini, flour, cornmeal, thyme, and salt and pepper to taste.

2. Melt the butter in a small saucepan over medium heat. Add the sweet fern and steep it in the butter until it becomes fragrant. Keep the butter warm over very low heat.

3. Coat the scallops in the cornmeal mixture, covering all surfaces.

4. Heat a medium nonstick skillet over medium-high heat. Add the olive oil to the skillet and swirl to heat it evenly. Sauté the scallops in the hot oil, flipping them once, for about 3 minutes on each side, or until the cornmeal crust turns a golden brown.

5. Turn the scallops out onto paper towels or brown paper bags to drain off some of the oil. Serve immediately, topped with the sweet fern butter sauce.

Braised Haddock with Summer Vegetables

2 cups dry white wine

1 cup Seafood Stock (page 65),
   or ½ fish bouillon cube
   dissolved in 1 cup boiling
   water

1 small zucchini, sliced

2 tender medium carrots,
   sliced

½ celery stalk, sliced

1 bouquet garni, or individual
   sprigs, of fresh thyme,
   oregano, sage, and a bay leaf

6 large haddock fillets,
   6 ounces each

Salt and freshly ground black
   pepper

Braising produces delicious results with just about any kind of whitefish, including the fresh haddock we eat so often in Nova Scotia. With this single dish consisting of fish, braised vegetables, and a savory sauce, you have an entire meal in minutes. A bouquet garni is a bundle of herbs—in this case, bay leaf, thyme, sage, and oregano—that are bound with twice or wrapped in cheesecloth and tied. The bouquet garni is always removed from a dish at the end of cooking or before service.

1. Combine the wine and stock in a large skillet, and bring to a boil. Simmer until slightly reduced, 10 minutes.

2. Add the zucchini, carrots, celery, and bouquet garni. Cook over medium heat until the vegetables are tender, 10 to 12 minutes. Using a slotted spoon, transfer the vegetables to a dish and discard the herbs.

3. Raise the heat under the skillet to medium-high and add the haddock fillets. The liquid should reach about halfway up the sides of the fillets; if needed, add more wine or stock to reach this level. Reduce the heat to a simmer, cover, and braise the fish, turning it once, until it just begins to flake, 7 to 8 minutes. Using a slotted spatula, transfer the fillets to warmed plates.

4. Raise the heat under the skillet to high, and cook until the liquid is reduced to a sauce-like consistency, about 5 minutes. Return the vegetables to the skillet, and add salt and pepper to taste. Stir until they are warmed through, 3 to 4 minutes.

5. Arrange the vegetables on and around the fillets, and spoon any remaining sauce over them. Serve immediately.

Casserole of Cherrystones, Artichokes, and Thyme

3 tablespoons plus
  2 teaspoons salt
8 small artichokes
¼ cup plus 2 tablespoons extra
  virgin olive oil
3 small sweet onions, sliced
6 garlic cloves, sliced
3 tablespoons dry red wine
2 tablespoons chopped green
  bell pepper
2 tablespoons chopped red
  bell pepper
½ cup long-grain white rice
2 pounds fresh cherrystone
  clams, scrubbed
8 sprigs fresh thyme
¼ cup dry white wine
2 ounces moist ricotta salata,
  cubed
¼ cup plus 2 tablespoons
  moist, plump raisins,
  preferably made from
  Muscatel grapes

Cherrystones are small clams whose sweet flavor contrasts pleasantly with the slight bitterness of artichokes and the savory notes of fresh thyme. For an attractive and easy tableside presentation, use a small glazed clay pot with a lid, like those found in Chinese groceries or from southern Spain. If you are using an unglazed clay pot, remember to soak the pot in cold water ahead of time to prevent it from drying too much and cracking in the oven. Serve a white Spanish Rioja or a French Muscadet with this dish.

1. Bring a large pot of water to a boil, and add 3 tablespoons of the salt. Lower the heat to a simmer and add the artichokes. Cook for 15 to 20 minutes, or until they are beginning to become tender. Remove the artichokes and cool them by running copious amounts of cold water over them. Set them aside to drain.

2. Heat 3 tablespoons of the olive oil in a sauté pan over medium-low heat. Add the onions and garlic, and sauté until caramelized, 10 to 12 minutes. Stir in the red wine, scraping up the browned bits at the bottom of the pan. Set it aside.

3. Trim the artichoke stems to a length of about 1 inch. Peel off the tough outer leaves of each artichoke. Slice off two-thirds of the artichoke top. Trim the heart with a knife until all that remains is the heart and a few tender leaves. (The artichokes and the caramelized onions can be prepared up to 4 hours in advance.)

4. Preheat the oven to 425° F.

5. Generously coat the inside of a glazed clay pot or ceramic casserole with the remaining 3 tablespoons of olive oil. Spread the caramelized onions and garlic in the bottom of the pot. Put in the artichokes, stems up. Add the bell pepper. Pour in the rice. Top with the clams and the thyme sprigs. Pour in the white wine. Scatter the cubes of ricotta salata over the other ingredients, and sprinkle with 2 teaspoons salt.

6. Cover the dish, transfer it to the oven, and bake for 12 minutes. Sprinkle the raisins over the top, and bake until the clams have opened and the rice is just done, 12 to 14 minutes. Allow it to cool for a few minutes. Serve hot.

Grilled Tuna with Sweet Red Pepper Sauce

SERVES 4

¼ cup extra virgin olive oil
Juice of ½ lemon
4 fresh tuna steaks, eight
  ounces each, 1 inch thick
Salt and freshly ground black
  pepper
Sweet Red Pepper Sauce
  (page 127)

Tomato-based red sauces are so commonplace that we sometimes forget that sweet red peppers also make for superb, rich, thick sauces with a style and flair all their own. We discovered this sauce while living in southern Spain and find it goes perfectly with fresh Nova Scotia seafood, especially with swordfish, shark, and, as featured here, the tuna that swim up to Atlantic Canada every year, following the Gulf Stream. The red peppers need to cook slowly in order to reach the soft consistency that makes for effortless sauce-making, so don't be impatient! We sometimes like to leave a little bit of the charred skin on, to add dimension to the flavor.

1. Mix the olive oil and lemon juice together in a baking dish. Add the tuna steaks and turn to coat them in the mixture. Cover and marinate for about 1 hour.

2. Prepare an outdoor grill or preheat the broiler.

3. Recoat the tuna steaks with the marinade, and season them with salt and pepper to taste. Grill over (or under) high heat for about 3 minutes on each side, or until done to your liking.

4. Serve the tuna with the sauce poured on top or next to the steaks.

Grilled Trout with Wild Fennel and Almonds

2 garlic cloves, chopped

¼ cup coarsely chopped
   blanched almonds

¼ cup plus 2 tablespoons extra
   virgin olive oil

1 teaspoon salt

¼ cup plus 2 tablespoons
   chopped wild fennel or
   domestic fennel fronds

3 large freshwater trout,
   cleaned and butterflied

In the spring, we fish for fresh brook trout right outside the Great Lodge on the Tusket River. In this dish, we combine a bit of Mediterranean influence—almonds and fennel—with the fish that gave the Lodge its name. Our guests enjoy this favorite meal while watching the river pass by, just a stone's throw away. Serve it with Wild Mushrooms en Papillote (page 6) and a dry white Bordeaux.

1. Using a food processor or a mortar and pestle, blend together the garlic, almonds, olive oil, salt, and fennel.

2. Remove as many bones as possible from the trout. Coat the inside of the trout with the fennel mixture and allow to marinate for about 1 hour.

3. Heat an indoor grill pan over high heat, or prepare an outdoor grill.

4. Grill the trout, skin side down, for 4 minutes. Turn the trout over and grill on the other side for another 4 minutes or until thoroughly cooked.

5. Slice the halves of the trout apart, and serve one half per person.

Trout Point Gumbos

Gumbo is perhaps Louisiana's most famous dish, at once both Creole and Cajun, although undoubtedly quintessentially urbane and Creole in its origins. It is traditionally enjoyed alongside homemade potato salad (try our version made with fresh lobster meat on page 91). Gumbo is like New Orleans's godchild: the city and the port combine to offer up layers of French technique, Afro-Caribbean spice, Native American ingenuity, and the seafood treasures of the Gulf. Gumbo evolved not only from the city's history of trade and commerce but also from the interaction between aristocratic and slave cultures. Black cooks, unable to find ingredients they had used in Africa, substituted others closer to hand in a process that produced new culinary sensibilities in a new world. When you taste gumbo, it is like tasting history.

Some notes on ingredients: We've found it's important to use unenriched flour when making a roux, as enriched flour can sometimes lend it a bitter taste. Traditional Creole recipes always use dried herbs and spices instead of fresh ones, a reflection of New Orleans's days as a trading port, when ingredients came in from distant lands by ship. To retain a true Creole taste, we always use dried seasonings in our gumbos.

Gumbo des Herbes (Green Gumbo)

½ cup safflower, peanut, or
canola oil

½ cup unbleached all-purpose
flour

½ onion, chopped

½ green bell pepper,
chopped

2 celery stalks, chopped

2 teaspoons minced garlic

4 cups Mushroom Stock
(page 46)

2 bay leaves

2 teaspoons dried thyme
leaves

1 teaspoon dried oregano

½ teaspoon cayenne
pepper

¼ teaspoon white pepper

2 pounds mixed greens:
mustard, turnip, collard,
chard, carrot tops, and/or
beet greens

1 fresh portobello mushroom,
sliced

Salt and freshly ground black
pepper

4 cups cooked white rice

A traditional Louisiana Lenten dish, *Gumbo des herbes* was a standard at our New Orleans eatery. This vegetarian soup has all the flavor and complexity of its seafood and meat cousins. You can use whatever leafy greens you have on hand—the more variety the better. We like to make a dark roux—almost black in color—for Gumbo des Herbes, as it adds more depth of flavor, though a paler, nutty brown roux will yield impressive results as well.

1. Prepare a dark roux: Heat the oil in a medium saucepan over high heat just until smoke rises from the surface. Sprinkle the flour over the hot oil and stir to blend it in thoroughly. Keep cooking and stirring until the mixture is very dark, 10 to 20 minutes.

2. Remove the pan from the heat and add the onion, bell pepper, celery, and garlic. Stir the vegetables into the roux, return the pan to medium heat, and cook until soft, 10 minutes.

3. Meanwhile, in a separate saucepan, heat the Mushroom Stock until it is almost simmering.

4. Slowly add the stock to the roux, stirring constantly, and bring it to a boil. Add the bay leaves, thyme, oregano, cayenne, and white pepper. Stir in the greens and the mushroom. Season with salt and pepper to taste, and simmer for 45 minutes.

5. Serve over hot white rice.

Trout Point's Seafood Gumbo

SERVES 6

1 teaspoon cayenne pepper

1 teaspoon white pepper

2 teaspoons freshly ground
black pepper

2 teaspoons dried thyme
leaves

1 teaspoon dried oregano

½ teaspoon ground allspice

½ teaspoon ground cloves

6 quahogs, or about 12 smaller
clams

12 shrimp, shelled and
deveined, shells reserved

½ cup canola or peanut oil

½ cup unbleached all-purpose
flour

3 celery stalks, chopped

2 medium yellow or white
onions, chopped

2 medium green bell peppers,
chopped

6 garlic cloves, minced

3 bay leaves

5 tablespoons Asian fish sauce
(see page 61)

6 cups Seafood Stock
(page 65)

There's something special about seafood gumbo. It's the prototypical New World dish, and nothing complements basic gumbo flavors better than our fresh Nova Scotia seafood. With a roux base, the Creole "trinity" of bell pepper, onion, and celery, plus other essential dried herbs and spices and a good stock, you can add a great variety of seafood.

1. In a small bowl, combine the cayenne, white pepper, black pepper, thyme, oregano, allspice, and cloves. Stir well and set aside.

2. Fill a large saucepan with water to a depth of ¾ inch. Bring to a boil over high heat. Add the quahogs and cover. Boil until the quahog shells just open, 3 to 8 minutes, taking out the quahogs as soon as they open, and leaving the others to continue cooking. Do not overcook them or the meat will become tough. Remove the meat from the shells and mince. Set aside. (The leftover boiling liquid can be strained and used as a seafood stock, such as for Finnan Haddie Jambalaya on page 152.)

3. Combine the reserved shrimp shells with about 1 cup water in a small saucepan and bring to a simmer. Cook until reduced to about ¾ cup, 12 minutes. Strain and set the shrimp water aside, discarding the shells.

4. Heat the oil in a heavy soup pot. When it is very hot, almost to the point of smoking, add the flour a bit at a time. Stir constantly to incorporate the flour into the oil while

Salt

12 fresh mussels, cleaned and
   debearded

2 fillets of halibut or other
   firm-fleshed fish, 8 ounces
   each

2 haddock fillets, 8 ounces
   each

6 cups cooked white rice

adjusting the heat to prevent burning. Continue stirring until the roux cooks to a very dark brown, almost black, color, 10 to 15 minutes.

5. Reduce the heat to low and add the celery. Cook until it starts to get tender, 2 to 3 minutes. Add the onions and cook until soft and translucent, 8 minutes. Finally add the bell peppers and garlic. Cook, stirring frequently, until the vegetables are soft, about 8 minutes. Add the bay leaves and about half of the seasoning mixture from step 1.

6. Add the fish sauce and the Seafood Stock, and bring to a simmer. Stir in the remaining seasoning mixture. Taste for flavor and adjust if necessary, adding salt to taste.

7. Add the minced quahogs and the mussels.

8. Add the reserved shrimp water to the gumbo.

7. Add the halibut and cook for 10 minutes.

9. Add the haddock and the shrimp, and cook for 3 minutes.

10. Serve immediately over scoops of hot white rice.

Seafood Gumbo II

1 pound medium shrimp, shelled and deveined, heads and shells reserved

½ cup canola or peanut oil

½ cup unbleached all-purpose flour

4 bay leaves

1½ cups chopped celery

2 cups chopped white or yellow onions

2 cups chopped green bell pepper

6 garlic cloves, finely chopped

5 cups Seafood Stock (page 65)

1 tablespoon dried oregano or marjoram

2 teaspoons dried thyme leaves

1 tablespoon onion powder

1½ teaspoons ground allspice

½ teaspoon ground cumin

4 whole cloves

1 tablespoon cayenne pepper

2 teaspoons freshly ground black pepper

This gumbo uses monkfish, sometimes referred to as anglerfish, which inhabits the waters off Nova Scotia in abundance and is found on both sides of the North Atlantic. We share the European adoration of this meaty, sweet, and very satisfying fish, known as "poor man's lobster" in local Acadian French communities. It is generally sold deheaded. You can skin it if you want and chop it into pieces, leaving the bone in for flavor.

1. Combine the shrimp shells and heads with 1 cup water in a small saucepan and bring to a simmer. Cook until reduced to ¼ cup, about 5 minutes. Strain and reserve the shrimp water, discarding the shells and heads.

2. Prepare a dark roux: Heat the oil in a medium saucepan over high heat almost to the point of smoking. Gradually add the flour, stirring constantly to blend it in thoroughly. Keep stirring until the mixture is very dark, 15 to 20 minutes.

3. Reduce the heat and add the bay leaves and celery. Cook until just tender, about 4 minutes.

4. Add the onions and cook until they begin to soften, 5 to 7 minutes. Then add the bell peppers and garlic and stir well.

5. Add the Seafood Stock and the shrimp water, and bring to a simmer. Stir in all the dried herbs and spices.

6. Add the monkfish pieces, and cook until tender but not falling apart, about 10 minutes.

7. Add the shrimp and the mussels, and cook just until the

1 teaspoon white pepper

Salt

1 small to medium monkfish,
2 to 2½ pounds, cut into
pieces

8 fresh mussels, cleaned and
debearded

6 cups cooked white rice

mussels open and the shrimp are done, 3 to 4 minutes.

8. Serve over hot white rice.

Making Roux

The cuisines of the French New World emerged from a multiethnic heritage and the antecedents of French-Canadian, Louisiana, Indian, Spanish, French, and Afro-Caribbean cooking.

The most elemental constituent in Louisiana cooking is the roux (which rhymes with "too")—a mixture of fat and flour. Every Creole and Cajun cook has his or her own way of making roux but the origins of Creole roux are still distinctly French. In classic French cuisine a roux is blond (though occasionally darker), made from equal parts fat and white flour, and used as a thickener for sauces, adding little flavor of its own. Over the centuries, however, Creole cooks transmogrified roux into something unique, toasting the flour in the oil to darker and darker complexions until, for some gumbos, an almost black roux was achieved. Creole roux has substantial flavor and aroma in addition to its thickening properties, and unlike the classic French version, is seldom blond. Creole recipes call for rouxs of almost every shade: light brown, peanut butter, red, dark brown, or even black.

The time it takes to cook roux can vary substantially. Cooking times to achieve a dark brown roux, for example, can vary from about 8 to about 25 minutes, with some cooks preferring very high heat, attempting to achieve a dark roux within minutes. The problem with this approach, especially for beginners, is the danger of burning the roux, which makes it bitter and unusable. It is important to always start with hot oil, just below the smoking point, before adding the flour in stages. It's also worth keeping in mind that adding the "Creole trinity"—celery, onions, and green bell pepper—to hot roux creates steam and thus more intense heat, which will cause the roux to darken further. If you have achieved nearly the color of roux desired, you can add the trinity, and the roux will darken to the desired point within a couple of minutes.

The Creole trinity is added to the hot roux along with traditional Creole seasonings. The Creole trinity is descendant from the classic French *mirepoix* and from the Spanish *sofrito* but, as with Creole roux, has been changed by history into something unique.

Some cooks prefer to add the trinity in stages, starting with the celery, moving on to the onions, and finishing with the bell pepper. Others like to add the trinity at different points in cooking a dish in order to achieve different textures and stages of doneness in the vegetables. The famous Louisiana chef Paul Prudhomme is a proponent of this technique, achieving layers of flavor and texture in a dish.

Roux may be stored in an airtight container in the refrigerator for up to two days, or frozen for up to one month, with or without the trinity added. The roux should be slowly reheated until hot before using it.

Fish and Mussel Bisque

SERVES 4

1½ pounds fresh mussels, cleaned and debearded

2 tablespoons unsalted butter

1 onion, chopped

1 large shallot, chopped

1 carrot, chopped

2 tomatoes, coarsely chopped

3 tablespoons chopped green bell pepper

1 celery stalk, finely chopped

2 garlic cloves, finely chopped

1 tablespoon chopped fresh flat-leaf parsley

This beautiful and satisfying dish—a meal unto itself—features the flavors of fresh seafood in abundance. If you like, reduce the amount of mussels and add other kinds of seafood, such as haddock or scallops.

1. Bring 5 cups of water to a boil in a large saucepan. Add the mussels. Boil until the mussel shells open, 4 to 6 minutes, taking the mussels out as soon as they open. Do not overcook them or the meat will become tough. Discard any that haven't opened. Remove the meat from the shells and set aside. Reserve 4 cups of the mussel water.

2. Melt the butter in a soup pot over medium heat. Add all the onion, shallot, carrot, tomatoes, pepper, and celery, a

1 tablespoon chopped fresh
   basil
1 teaspoon chopped fresh
   tarragon
Salt and freshly ground black
   pepper
White pepper
Seafood Stock (page 65),
   if needed
¼ cup dry vermouth
1 pound sole fillets
1 cup heavy cream

little bit at a time. Stir in the garlic. Cook until the vegetables are soft and the onion is translucent, 8 to 10 minutes.

3. Add the parsley, basil, tarragon, salt to taste, and black and white pepper to taste. Add the 4 cups reserved mussel steaming water (if you don't have enough, supplement it with Seafood Stock). Bring to a simmer. Lower the heat and add the vermouth, mussels, and sole.

4. Remove the pot from the heat and stir the cream into the bisque. Serve immediately.

Sesame and Dill–Encrusted Haddock

SERVES 6

1 cup unbleached all-purpose
   flour
½ cup sesame seeds
Salt and freshly ground black
   pepper
1 tablespoon dried dill leaves
3 eggs
3 tablespoons whole milk
Canola oil
6 haddock fillets, 6 ounces
   each
Thyme and Dill Cream Sauce
   (recipe follows)

1. Combine the flour, sesame seeds, salt and pepper to taste, and dill in a small mixing bowl.

2. In a separate bowl, whisk the eggs and milk together.

3. Pour the oil into a large skillet to a depth of 1 inch and heat over medium heat.

4. Rinse the fillets under cold water. Coat them in the egg/milk mixture, and then dredge them in the flour mixture, coating the fillets evenly, without clumps.

5. Sauté the fillets in the hot oil for 2 to 5 minutes on each side. Do not overcook.

6. Coat with Thyme and Dill Cream Sauce, and serve.

Thyme and Dill Cream Sauce

MAKES ABOUT ¾ CUP

2 sprigs fresh thyme

1 bay leaf

3 tablespoons chopped
   shallots or scallions (white
   and light green parts only)

1½ cups dry white wine

1 cup heavy cream

Salt and freshly ground black
   pepper

1 tablespoon dried dill leaves

1. Combine the thyme, bay leaf, shallots, and wine in a saucepan and bring to a simmer. Cook until reduced to ¼ cup, about 20 minutes. Set the pan aside.

2. Pour the cream into a small saucepan and bring it to a boil. Cook until reduced to ⅓ cup, 15 to 20 minutes. Remove the thyme sprigs and bay leaf from the reduced wine mixture, and whisk the wine mixture into the cream. Add salt and pepper to taste.

3. Simmer this mixture over low heat for 2 to 3 minutes, and then stir in the dill.

4. Serve the sauce immediately to prevent separation. If the sauce does separate, reheat slowly and gently whisk in a little more cream.

Perch and Hake Courtbouillon

SERVES 6

¾ cup canola oil

¾ cup unbleached all-purpose
   flour

1½ pounds fresh tomatoes,
   chopped

6 ounces (1 can) tomato paste

2 celery stalks, finely
   chopped

1 small onion, chopped

1 green bell pepper, chopped

Ah, "courtbouillon." Although it looks as though it belongs in the repertoire of classical French cookery (which in some ways it does), Creole courtbouillon is a very different creature from its Old World ancestor. The single similarity is that the fish is simmered in a mixture of vegetables and wine or vermouth. In this distinctly Creole dish, tomatoes figure prominently, as does a reddish-colored roux. This is our favorite version, but as with all Creole dishes, there are as many varia-

5 cups Seafood Stock
   (page 65) or water
8 ounces fresh mushrooms,
   sliced, optional
8 garlic cloves, minced
3 bay leaves
½ teaspoon dried thyme leaves
½ teaspoon ground allspice
1 teaspoon cayenne pepper
Freshly ground black pepper
White pepper
1 lemon, thinly sliced
Salt
2 large perch fillets, 6 to
   8 ounces each, cut into
   large pieces
3 large hake fillets, cut into
   large pieces
1 cup dry red wine, or ½ cup
   dry vermouth, or to taste
6 cups cooked white rice

tions as there are cooks. Feel free to vary or omit ingredients, make a lighter roux, and add as little or as much wine as you want.

1. Prepare a dark roux: Heat the canola oil in a medium saucepan over high heat almost to the point of smoking. Gradually add the flour, stirring constantly to blend it in thoroughly. Keep stirring until the mixture is very dark, 15 to 20 minutes.

2. Stir in the chopped tomatoes and tomato paste, and cook over medium-low heat for 10 minutes. If the mixture is too dry, add ¼ cup of water.

3. Add the celery, onion, and bell pepper, and cook over medium heat until tender, 5 minutes.

4. Add the Seafood Stock, mushrooms, garlic, bay leaves, thyme, allspice, cayenne, black pepper to taste, white pepper to taste, and lemon slices. Bring to a boil, reduce the heat, and simmer for 30 minutes. Taste, and adjust the seasonings, adding salt if needed.

5. Add the perch, hake, and wine, and simmer for 5 minutes. Remove the bay leaves. Serve over hot white rice.

Haddock Fillets Amandine

½ cup semolina flour

Salt and freshly ground black
pepper

6 haddock fillets, 6 to
8 ounces each, or 12
smaller fillets

5 tablespoons unsalted butter,
or more as needed

½ cup slivered blanched
almonds

Juice of 2 lemons, strained

¼ cup coarsely chopped fresh
parsley, optional

There isn't a more classic Haute Creole preparation than *amandine.* It's easy once you get the hang of working fast—you have to cook the fish and make the sauce within a couple of minutes of each other—but the sauce is so simple and so good, it's irresistible. We also love making this dish with sea trout fillets, in which case you should soak the fillets in milk for half an hour before dredging them with the flour. Sole is also wonderful prepared this way.

1. Put the semolina flour on a plate and season it with salt and pepper to taste.

2. Dredge the fish fillets in the flour mixture.

3. Heat a skillet over medium-high heat, and add the butter. Cook the fillets, flipping them only once, 4 minutes on each side. The semolina crust should brown. Place the cooked fillets on a warmed serving platter or individual plates.

4. There should be enough butter remaining in the skillet to form a sauce. If not, add more butter.

5. Raise the heat to high under the skillet. Toss the almonds in the butter until toasted, 1 minute. Immediately add the lemon juice. Reduce the mixture over high heat until it has a sauce-like consistency, about 30 seconds.

6. Spoon some of the almond mixture over each fillet. Serve immediately, topped with the optional chopped parsley.

Shrimp Creole

½ cup canola or peanut oil

½ cup unbleached all-purpose flour

1½ cups chopped celery

2 cups chopped white onions

2 cups chopped green bell peppers

¼ cup plus 2 tablespoons minced garlic

4 bay leaves

6 medium ripe tomatoes, chopped

1½ cups Seafood Stock (page 65) or water, heated, as needed

12 ounces shrimp, shelled and deveined, shells and heads reserved

2 dashes hot pepper sauce, such as Tabasco or Crystal

2 teaspoons Worcestershire sauce

1 tablespoon dried ground oregano

1 tablespoon dried oregano leaves

1½ teaspoons dried thyme leaves

Served here with fresh shrimp, Creole sauce can complement a variety of different foods (including eggs for breakfast). The use of a roux base, fresh tomatoes, the "trinity," and bay leaf distinguishes this dish as a truly Creole creation. We've added a few ingredients, such as shrimp stock and fish sauce, that deepen the flavor.

1. Heat the canola oil in a small, heavy-bottomed stockpot over medium heat. When the oil is very hot, reduce the heat to medium-low and add the flour, stirring constantly to incorporate it into the oil. It will sizzle at first and then, as it cooks, slowly darken in color. Cook the flour, stirring constantly, until it turns peanut butter–colored, 12 to 14 minutes, adjusting the heat as necessary to prevent burning. Cook for a few minutes more until it starts to take on a ruddy cast.

2. Stir the celery into the roux and cook until just tender, about 4 minutes. Add the onions and cook until soft, about 8 minutes. Add the bell peppers, half of the garlic, and the bay leaves and cook 4 minutes longer.

3. Add the tomatoes and cook for 7 minutes over medium-low heat. You may want to add about ½ cup Seafood Stock or water to facilitate the softening of the tomatoes.

4. Combine the shrimp shells and heads with ¾ cup water in a small saucepan. Bring to a boil and cook until reduced to ½ cup liquid, about 15 minutes. Pour the shrimp stock through a strainer into the roux mixture, and stir.

1 teaspoon cayenne pepper,
  or to taste
½ teaspoon freshly ground
  black pepper
¼ teaspoon white pepper
1 tablespoon ground allspice
1 tablespoon hot paprika
1 tablespoon salt, or to taste
1 teaspoon sugar, optional
  (omit if the vegetables have
  enough natural sweetness)
¼ cup Asian fish sauce
  (see page 61)
6 cups cooked white rice

5. Stir in the hot pepper sauce and Worcestershire sauce. Add the dried herbs and spices, and simmer until the tomatoes soften and the consistency is sauce-like, 20 to 30 minutes. Taste, and adjust the seasonings and salt as needed. Add more stock or water if the sauce is too thick.

6. Add the shrimp and cook them in the sauce until pink, 5 minutes. Stir in the remaining 3 tablespoons garlic and the fish sauce. Remove from the heat and serve over hot white rice.

Crawfish and Carrot Jambalaya

3 tablespoons extra virgin
   olive oil or peanut oil

1½ onions, coarsely chopped

1 green bell pepper, chopped

½ celery stalk, chopped

2 tablespoons chopped fresh
   parsley

2 bay leaves, preferably fresh

2 teaspoons sea salt

1 teaspoon dried thyme leaves

1 teaspoon dried marjoram

½ teaspoon freshly ground
   black pepper

½ teaspoon cayenne pepper

½ teaspoon white pepper

1 teaspoon dried basil,
   optional

1 pinch saffron threads

12 baby carrots

12 ounces peeled crawfish tails

1 cup long-grain white rice

About 2½ cups Chicken Stock
   (page 60), Seafood Stock
   (page 65), or Mushroom
   Stock (page 46)

The fresh baby carrots in this jambalaya accent the sweet, earthy flavors of the crawfish.

1. Preheat the oven to 425° F.

2. Put the oil in a paella pan or a wide, ovenproof skillet, spreading it over the surface.

3. In a large mixing bowl, thoroughly combine all the remaining ingredients except the stock.

4. Place the ingredients in the pan, and add enough stock to just cover the surface of the mixture.

5. Cover, and bake for 15 minutes. Remove the lid and bake for another 25 minutes, or until the rice is tender. Serve immediately.

Paella-Jambalaya

¼ cup peanut oil

¼ cup unbleached all-purpose flour

1 cup chopped onions

1 cup chopped green bell peppers

1 cup chopped red bell peppers

2 celery stalks, chopped

1 large tomato, coarsely chopped

4 bay leaves

½ cup extra virgin olive oil

5 whole cloves

⅛ teaspoon ground cloves

2 tablespoons minced garlic

3½ teaspoons dried thyme leaves

1 teaspoon dried marjoram

2 teaspoons sea salt

1 teaspoon cayenne pepper

1 teaspoon freshly ground black pepper

¼ teaspoons ground coriander

½ teaspoon ground cumin

8 ounces smoked haddock or other smoked whitefish, such as pollock, cut into 2-inch chunks

We took the old adage that "jambalaya is the Creole world's paella" to heart when we devised this Creole-seasoned version. We also added a little bit of dark roux to give the mixture extra richness. Made on the stovetop, this hearty rice dish should be cooked in a paella pan or a deep sauté pan. The technique of covering the paella after removing it from the heat ensures that the rice is perfectly cooked.

1. Heat the peanut oil in a paella pan or a large deep skillet over high heat. When it is very hot, gradually add the flour, stirring constantly to blend it in. Keep stirring until the mixture is dark brown, 18 minutes.

2. Add ½ cup of the onions, ½ cup each of the bell peppers, and half the celery to the roux. Sauté over medium heat, stirring frequently, until softened, about 10 minutes. (You may prepare this up to 4 hours in advance.)

3. Add the tomato and cook for 5 minutes. Then add the bay leaves, olive oil, whole and ground cloves, garlic, thyme, marjoram, salt, cayenne, black pepper, coriander, and cumin. Stir until fragrant, about 3 minutes.

4. Stir in the smoked haddock and cook until fragrant, about 2 minutes. Add 3½ cups of the stock and bring to a simmer.

5. Stir in the shrimp, clams, scallops, and mussels. Add the remaining ½ cup of onion and ½ cup each of the bell peppers, and the remaining half of the celery. Add the rice and the fish sauce, and stir until thoroughly mixed. Cook the

About 5 cups Seafood Stock
(page 65) or shrimp water
(reserved from another
recipe)

6 large shrimp, shelled and
deveined

6 fresh clams, scrubbed

6 large fresh sea scallops

6 fresh mussels, cleaned and
debearded

1⅞ cups long-grain white rice

2 tablespoons Asian fish sauce
(see page 61)

jambalaya over low to medium-low heat for 25 minutes, or until all of the liquid has been absorbed and the rice is just less than al dente. As it cooks, add more stock as needed to keep the mixture from burning.

6. Remove the pan from the heat and let the jambalaya stand, covered with a clean dish towel, until the rice is al dente, 10 minutes. Pick out the bay leaves and whole cloves before serving, if desired.

Finnan Haddie Jambalaya

¼ cup extra virgin olive oil

1 cup chopped onions

1 cup chopped green bell
   peppers

1 cup chopped celery

4 bay leaves

3 whole cloves

2 tablespoons minced garlic

2 teaspoons dried thyme
   leaves

1 teaspoon sea salt

1 teaspoon cayenne pepper

1 teaspoon freshly ground
   black pepper

1 teaspoon filé powder

½ teaspoon ground cumin

8 ounces fresh sea scallops,
   cut in half

8 ounces smoked haddock
   fillets (finnan haddie) or
   other smoked whitefish,
   such as pollock, cut into
   2-inch pieces

8 fresh mussels, cleaned and
   debearded

1 cup long-grain white
   rice

Finnan haddie—or smoked haddock fillets—originated in Findon, a fishing community near Aberdeen, Scotland. Their popularity soon spread the world over, including Nova Scotia and France. We make our "haddies" in the Lodge smokehouse, following age-old methods, salting the fillets first and then smoking them until they turn a beautiful pale gold. The tempting smoky flavor of finnan haddie makes it an unbeatable substitute for andouille sausage in many of our Creole dishes at the Lodge—we add the smoked haddock early in the cooking process to allow the full smoky flavor to permeate the dish.

Filé Powder

Filé powder, an integral ingredient in Creole cooking, is made from ground dried sassafras leaves. It acts as a thickener for stews in addition to possessing its own herbaceous flavor. Filé entered the Creole culinary repertoire from the Native American culture of southern Louisiana.

1. Preheat the oven to 375° F.
2. Heat the olive oil in a large enameled cast-iron casserole. Add the onions, bell peppers, and celery, and cook over moderate heat, stirring occasionally, until softened, about 8 minutes.

2 cups bottled clam juice or shrimp water (reserved from another recipe)

1 tablespoon Worcestershire sauce

3. Add the bay leaves, cloves, garlic, thyme, salt, cayenne, black pepper, filé powder, and cumin. Cook, stirring, until fragrant, about 3 minutes.

4. Stir in the scallops, smoked fish, mussels, and rice. Add the clam juice, 2½ cups of water, and the Worcestershire sauce. Cover and bring to a simmer.

5. Transfer the casserole to the oven and bake the jambalaya until all of the liquid has been absorbed, 25 minutes. Add a little water if it begins to look too dry.

6. Let the jambalaya stand, covered, for 10 minutes. Pick out the bay leaves and cloves before serving, if desired.

Tuna Empanada

1/4 cup plus 2 tablespoons extra
   virgin olive oil

2 1/4 pounds tomatoes, chopped

1 or 2 small dried red chile
   peppers, such as pepperoncino

1 teaspoon freshly ground
   black pepper

2 teaspoons sea salt

1 tablespoon sugar

1 cup chopped onions

1/4 cup chopped small fresh
   sweet red chile peppers,
   or grilled red bell peppers

8 3/4 ounces high-quality
   canned tuna, such as bonito

14 ounces frozen puff pastry
   dough, thawed

1 egg, beaten with 1 teaspoon
   water

1. Heat 2 tablespoons of the olive oil in a medium skillet over medium heat. Add the chopped tomatoes, red chili peppers, black pepper, salt, and sugar. Cook over low heat for 30 minutes. Strain the mixture through a food mill, or blend it in a food processor. Set the sauce aside in a large bowl.

2. In a separate skillet, heat the remaining 1/4 cup olive oil over medium heat. Add the chopped onions and cook until golden, about 12 minutes. Mix the onions, the sweet red peppers, and the tuna into the tomato sauce.

3. Preheat the oven to 375° F.

4. Divide the puff pastry into two equal pieces, and roll them out on a lightly floured work surface to form thin sheets measuring about 11 by 8 inches. Spread a small amount of flour on a baking sheet, and place one sheet of puff pastry on it.

5. Using a rubber spatula, spread the filling evenly over the pastry, leaving a 1/2-inch edge all around. Brush the egg wash over the exposed edge. Place the second sheet of pastry on top, and press the edges together, sealing the empanada.

6. Bake until the pastry is golden and flaky, 20 minutes.

Tuna Daube

3 tablespoons capers

3 tablespoons whole pink or
black peppercorns

10 garlic cloves, finely chopped

6 anchovy fillets packed in oil

Sea salt

4 tablespoons extra virgin
olive oil, plus extra for the
tuna

3 green bell peppers, char-
grilled and peeled
(see page 60)

3 red bell peppers, char-grilled
and peeled (see page 60)

One 4-pound tuna loin, or
4 pounds tuna steaks,
cut about 1 inch thick

2 tablespoons freshly cracked
black pepper

5 onions, cut in half and sliced

4 lovage stalks

6 lemon thyme sprigs

2 French thyme sprigs

2 fresh sage leaves

Zest of 2 lemons, removed
with a vegetable peeler and
cut into matchstick-size
pieces

Daube glacée, another classic Creole dish from New Orleans, is usually made with beef. Here we substitute meaty tuna for this roast redolent with the aromas of black pepper, lovage, and garlic. This dish is excellent served on couscous or steamed millet.

1. Rinse the capers and set them aside to drain.
2. Using a mortar and pestle, mash together the peppercorns, garlic, anchovy fillets, 1 teaspoon salt, and 1 tablespoon of the olive oil. Set the mixture aside.
3. Seed the grilled peppers and cut them into ½-inch-wide slices. Set them aside.
4. Coat the tuna loin with olive oil and press the pepper onto it. Heat a large heavy skillet or indoor grill pan over high heat. Add the tuna and sear the outside, about 1 minute on each side. Set it aside.
5. Preheat the oven to 350° F.
6. Heat a large cast-iron pot or casserole over medium heat, add the remaining 3 tablespoons olive oil, and sauté the onions until softened, 10 minutes. Add the herbs, lemon zest, and the peppercorn mixture from step 2. Toss with a spatula. Then add the wine and simmer for 10 minutes. Add the fish sauce and optional sugar.
7. Place the tuna loin in the casserole and cover it with the pepper slices, tomatoes, capers, and pepperoncino chiles. Season with salt to taste. Cover, transfer the pot to the oven, and bake for 30 minutes.

2 cups dry white wine, such
as a dry Chardonnay or
Sauvignon Blanc

3 tablespoons Asian fish sauce
(see page 61)

2 tablespoons sugar, optional

One 32-ounce can diced plum
tomatoes

5 dried pepperoncino chile
peppers, crumbled

8. Remove the herb sprigs. Slice the tuna loin and serve, each portion covered with the sauce.

Pâté à la Rapure (Rappie Pie)

2 pounds russet potatoes,
peeled

1 cup Chicken Stock (page 60),
Seafood Stock (page 65),
or bottled clam juice

2 medium onions, finely
chopped

Salt and freshly ground black
pepper

1 teaspoon chopped fresh
thyme

¼ teaspoon cayenne pepper

6 tablespoons (¾ stick)
unsalted butter, at room
temperature

12 fresh cherrystone clams,
shucked and coarsely
chopped, ½ cup clam liquid
reserved

8 ounces fresh sea scallops,
cut into 1-inch pieces

Rappie Pie is to Acadian cooking what gumbo or étouffée is to Cajun cuisine. Like Cajun dishes, it is made from common, inexpensive ingredients, often with freshly caught seafood. Pressing all the starch from the grated potatoes leaves the protein—a practice unique to Acadian cuisine that lends unusual texture and flavor to the dish.

1. Preheat the oven to 400° F. Butter a medium glass or ceramic baking dish.

2. Coarsely grate the potatoes. Transfer them to a coarse stainless-steel sieve, and using a spatula, press on the potatoes to extract as much liquid as possible.

3. Heat the stock in a skillet over medium heat. Add the potatoes and cook until thick, about 3 minutes. Remove the skillet from the heat and stir in half of the onions, a large pinch of salt, 1 teaspoon pepper, ½ teaspoon of the thyme, and the cayenne. Set the mixture aside.

4. Melt 2 tablespoons of the butter in a medium skillet over low heat. Add the remaining onion and the remaining ½ teaspoon thyme, and cook until the onion softens, about 8 minutes. Add the reserved ½ cup of clam liquid and bring to a boil. Cook over high heat until the liquid is reduced by half, about 3 minutes.

5. Remove the skillet from the heat and let the mixture cool slightly. Then stir in the clams and scallops, and season with salt and pepper.

6. Spread half of the potato mixture in a layer in the prepared baking dish. Spread the onions, clams, and scallops on top. Cover with the remaining potatoes. Dot the top of the pie with the remaining 4 tablespoons butter, in small pieces, and bake until bubbling hot, 45 minutes.

7. Preheat the broiler.

8. Broil the pie for 3 minutes, or until it is browned and crisp on top. Let it stand for 10 minutes before serving.

Chapter six

Breads

Some masons and stone workers built a baking oven, with which we make for ourselves bread as good as that in Paris.

—Marc Lescarbot, *Histoire de la Nouvelle-France,* 1609

Freshly baked breads accompany every meal at Trout Point Lodge. Canada produces some of the world's finest grains, and we gladly take advantage of them, following Acadian French baking traditions. Every early Acadian homestead had a big stone-lined bake oven, and every French Nova Scotian we know speaks fondly of the big stoves that warmed the entire house throughout the harsh, blustery winters. Unlike the European Old World, and even our native New Orleans, bakeries did not exist, and all bread for meals came from the home.

We produce a variety of breads at the Lodge. Cooking different meals for our guests gives us a chance to try out and refine new bread recipes and bread-making techniques. If you are new to bread making, start with the Rye-Hempseed Bread or the Green Olive Round, both of which involve store-bought yeast dissolved in warm water, simple ingredients, and kneading, and both of which can be made in a matter of hours. Don't be afraid to experiment by kneading for more or less time or by varying the moisture of the dough—this is how you will learn how the bread dough should look and feel to produce the desired result. Always start the learning process by hand-kneading your breads, to get a good sense of what dough feels like, and then progress to using a mixer with a dough hook, which will save time and allows for multitasking in the kitchen. Since we don't have a specialty baker, we usually have to make bread and prepare one or more other dishes simultaneously—so we know the value of the mixer for a busy cook!

The Starter

We call this a "wild yeast" starter because we capture native yeast spores flying around the kitchen to produce an active starter. This starter, also referred to as sourdough starter, is a type of active yeast mixture to keep on hand for making special breads. A starter such as this lends better flavor and texture to almost any kind of wheat flour–based bread.

You may ask: Why go to the trouble of making a wild yeast starter?

First, because the flavor it produces in the finished bread is marvelous: deep, a little sour, and complex. The texture and structure of the breads is also better: chewier and crustier. Second, because it makes your breads unique—just like the famous "San Francisco Sourdough." Capturing and using indigenous wild yeasts makes for breads that are unique to their locale. The wild yeast breads we made in Mount Hermon, Louisiana, for example, were very different in flavor and texture from the ones we now make in Kemptville, Nova Scotia—even though the recipe itself is exactly the same. Third, in our experience, wild yeast breads also last longer without turning stale, remaining delicious for several days instead of one or two.

Wild Yeast Starter

About 7 cups unbleached
all-purpose flour or whole
wheat flour, or a mixture of
the two

1 apple, unpeeled, cut into
8 wedges

This wild yeast starter can be retained for years, even decades, by simply "feeding" it on a regular basis. It's called a "mother" culture because it acts as the progenitor for many breads over a long period of time.

The skin on the apple slices helps wild yeast grow on this starter.

1. In a medium ceramic or glass mixing bowl, blend 4 cups of the flour with about 3 cups water—enough to make a very liquid mixture. (Mix, rather than knead, since you are not creating bread dough but simply a culture medium for the yeast.) The starter should have the consistency of porridge.

2. Add the apple wedges, submerging them in the starter mixture.

3. Allow the bowl to sit out in the kitchen, ideally in a warm (but not hot) place, for 2 days. Do not cover it, since you want the mixture to capture wild yeast spores in the air. If a crust forms on top, simply stir the starter once a day.

4. After the 2 days, remove and discard 1½ cups of the starter. Stir in 1 cup fresh flour and ½ cup water. Leave the bowl, uncovered, for 2 or 3 days, at which point the starter will have risen and you should see bubbles starting to appear in the mixture.

5. Repeat this step until the starter has thoroughly bubbled and risen at least three times. Remove the apple wedges.

6. At this point, you may refrigerate the starter in a ceramic or glass bowl loosely covered with plastic wrap; the cold will keep the yeast alive without your having to constantly "feed"

it. Each time you use some of the starter, feed the "mother" by replacing what you have removed with an equal amount of mixed flour and water. Be sure to feed the starter every 5 days, whether you're using it or not. Mother starters of this type can live for years.

Kneading

Without proper kneading, breads will lack structure and "crumb," which refers to the inner part of the bread, within the crust. Mindlessly following time recommendations for kneading, without paying attention to how the dough is developing, will result in unsatisfactory breads. Changing conditions—relative humidity, altitude, flour quality—can have dramatic effects on how a recipe functions.

The more kneading you do (up to a point), the better the structure of the resulting bread. But in addition to proper kneading, the "rest" is important for a developing bread dough. Gluten, the proteinaceous element that builds structure in wheat breads, develops just *after* you finish kneading. By giving a rest period of 5 to 10 minutes after your first kneading, you allow time for the gluten to develop, creating better structure for the loaf. Without this rest period, your kneading will be less effective.

As you knead, pay attention to how the dough feels, how it holds together, and how easily it breaks or stretches when pulled. The better developed the dough, the more elastic it will be—it will not break apart easily, and you can often form a very thin sheet of dough that is almost translucent. When the dough has developed to this point, it is ready for rising. If you were to knead beyond this point, it would cause the gluten structure to break down, which would yield unsatisfactory results.

Salt

Salt is critical to the flavor of any kind of bread. Some flours, such as rye, take quite a bit of salt. But salt also can retard yeast growth. Therefore we often allow some time for the yeast and dough to develop before adding salt to the mix, usually after a short rest. But don't forget to add the amount of salt specified in the recipe, or you'll have a dull, less flavorful bread.

Moisture

Moisture plays an extremely important role in the development, rising, and ultimate texture of breads. In flatbreads, like our Garden Herb Bread, extra moisture results in an excellent open crumb and chewy texture. In larger loaves, however, this much moisture can make the dough very difficult to handle, impossible to shape properly, and ultimately weak in structure. Experiment with different moisture levels in your dough, and with varying the shape of the loaf, to produce different effects and textures. Loaf shape and moisture level work in conjunction to determine the character of the bread.

Hand-forming Versus Loaf Pans

At times, hand-forming a loaf makes a lot of sense, such as when you want a particular shape or more crust, or when you want the bread to rise in a certain way. For everyday baking, however, do not feel that you are cutting corners by using a loaf pan. Almost any bread can be minimally shaped and then put into a loaf pan for baking with superb results. The nonstick pans work extremely well and clean up very easily.

In hand-forming bread, work or fold the dough so that an exterior skin—the eventual crust—is created. Remember that the ways in which you twist and turn the dough before baking will affect how well the dough rises and the ultimate shape it will take. Focus on filling the "skin" with as much height and structure as possible, which is in turn determined by how and in what direction you work the dough. Usually you should work the dough from the bottom of the loaf up toward the top of the loaf and out.

To hand-form baguettes, first use the palms of your hands to flatten the dough into thin rectangles the length of the desired baguette. Fold over each side, using about 1 inch of dough. Press down on the newly created seams in the dough to completely seal them. Gently roll the dough, as you would a rolling pin, to create a rounded baguette shape, always keeping the desired length. If you have the special rounded baking pans for baguettes, grease them and then place the dough into them. Otherwise, allow the dough to rise on a flat, floured baking sheet. In this case, you may have baguettes with one flat side, but they will taste just as good!

Steam

We almost always toss half a cup of water into our oven when we begin baking a loaf of bread. This produces copious amounts of steam, which results in a better, thicker crust on the loaves. You can repeat this step once again during baking to maintain constant steam. Some people place ice cubes or containers of water in the oven during baking, but we find that our method works best.

Whole Wheat Flax Baguettes

MAKES 2 LARGE BAGUETTES

¾ cup Wild Yeast Starter
   (page 163)
3 teaspoons active dry yeast
½ cup rye flour
½ cup unbleached all-purpose
   flour
4 cups stone-ground whole
   wheat flour
½ cup flaxseed
1 tablespoon salt

1. In a medium ceramic or glass mixing bowl, mix together the Wild Yeast Starter, the yeast, and ½ cup warm water. When the yeast has dissolved, add the three flours, flaxseed, and salt. Add about 1½ cups warm water, mixing until a dough develops.

2. Knead the dough by hand on a lightly floured surface, or with a heavy-duty electric mixer fitted with the dough hook, for 20 to 25 minutes, or until the dough is thoroughly elastic and stretchy.

3. Cover the bowl with a damp cloth and let the dough rise until it has doubled in bulk, about 3 hours in a warm kitchen or 5 hours at cooler room temperature.

4. Stretch the dough and flip it over. Like punching down dough, stretching both deflates the dough and helps the gluten to develop. Cover the bowl again and allow the dough to rise until it has doubled in bulk again, about 2 hours.

5. Divide the dough in half and form each portion into a baguette (see page 165). Allow the baguettes to rise for 20 minutes.

6. While the dough is rising, preheat the oven to 425° F.

7. Place the baking sheet or baguette pans in the oven and bake until the loaves are browned on top, about 25 minutes.

Spelt Raisin-Walnut Bread

MAKES 1 LOAF

2⅔ cups whole milk

5 teaspoons active dry yeast

1 cup spelt flour or whole wheat flour

2 cups stone-ground white flour

1 cup unbleached all-purpose flour

1½ teaspoons salt

2 cups sultana (golden) or black raisins

1 cup walnut pieces

Cornmeal

This bread combines hearty whole wheat flavors with the flawless combination of walnuts and raisins.

1. Heat the milk in a medium saucepan until scalded. Set it aside to cool to lukewarm.

2. Stir the yeast into ¼ cup warm water until it dissolves.

3. Combine the three flours and the salt in a large mixing bowl or in the bowl of an electric mixer, and stir well. Add the yeast mixture. Slowly incorporate 2 cups of the scalded milk. Add more milk as needed to form a firm but pliable dough.

4. Knead the dough by hand on a lightly floured surface or in the mixer for 5 minutes. Allow it to rest for 5 minutes. Then knead it for 10 minutes, or until a consistent, slightly stretchy dough has formed.

5. Flatten the dough out on a lightly floured work surface into a rough rectangle. Add the raisins and nuts, pressing them into the dough with the palms of your hands. Roll the dough up and form it into a ball. Place the ball in a large bowl and cover. Allow the dough to rise until almost doubled in bulk (the raisins and nuts will weight it down somewhat), 4 to 5 hours.

6. Preheat the oven to 390° F. Dust a baking sheet with cornmeal.

7. Form the dough into a thick cylinder or rectangle, and place it on the prepared baking sheet. Allow it to rise for another 25 minutes, or until the dough springs back firmly when pressed with the tip of your finger.

8. Bake for 40 minutes, or until a brown crust forms. Place the loaf on a wire rack to cool for at least 20 minutes before cutting.

Rye-Hempseed Bread

MAKES 1 LOAF

1 tablespoon active dry yeast

3 cups stone-ground rye flour

1½ cups unbleached all-purpose flour

½ cup hempseed flour

8 tablespoons olive oil, plus extra for the pan

1 tablespoon salt

5 tablespoons caraway seeds

Along with many other specialty crops, hemp has regained stature among Canadian farmers. When we saw beautifully green hempseed flour on the grocer's shelf on a trip to Halifax, we knew we had to try it. Hempseed flour is more a special additive than the basis for a bread, and the best results occur when the finely milled hempseeds are blended with stone-ground rye flour. The final product is a loaf with deep flavors, great for eating plain or serving with cheese. You can easily make this bread without an electric mixer, as it does not require much kneading.

1. Stir the yeast into ¼ cup warm water in a medium mixing bowl, until it dissolves.

2. Blend the three flours together in a bowl, and add them to the yeast mixture. Add 2 tablespoons of the olive oil. Slowly mix in more warm water, 1 to 1½ cups, until a firm but somewhat tacky dough develops.

3. Knead the dough on a lightly floured surface for 5 minutes. Let it rest for 5 minutes. Sprinkle the salt and the caraway seeds on top, and knead for another 5 minutes.

4. Cover the dough and let it rise, turning it over once, for about 1 hour.

5. Punch the dough down and knead it for about 2 minutes. Then form it into a loaf shape.

Liberally coat a loaf pan with olive oil, and place the dough in the pan. Cover and allow it to rise for about 25 minutes.

6. Meanwhile preheat the oven to 390° F.

7. Brush the remaining 6 tablespoons olive oil over the dough, and bake for about 40 minutes, or until the loaf sounds hollow when tapped with your knuckles. Remove from the pan and cool on a wire rack.

Tusket Brown Whole-Grain Bread

MAKES 2 LOAVES

2 cups Wild Yeast Starter (page 163), or 2½ tablespoons of active dry yeast

2 cups spelt flour

5 cups stone-ground whole wheat flour

½ cup stone-ground rye flour

1½ cups unbleached all-purpose flour or stone-ground white flour

½ cup flaxseed

¼ cup cracked wheat

3 tablespoons wheat bran

3 tablespoons salt

Cornmeal

The rich brown colors in this bread remind us of the peat-filtered waters of the Tusket River, which flows by just a stone's throw from the dining room. We typically use a sourdough starter for this bread, which lends deep flavor and gives it great shelf life, but you can substitute store-bought yeast. The loaf combines the rich flavors and textures of spelt, regular wheat, and rye flours with generous proportions of flaxseed and other grains. The topping of cornmeal makes for *pan* perfection! We usually form these loaves into round or oval shapes, but loaf pans work fine as well.

1. If you are using sourdough starter, mix it with 1 cup warm water in a large bowl. If you are using yeast, stir it into ½ cup warm water in a large bowl until it dissolves.

2. Add the four flours to the starter. Then stir in about 3 cups warm water—just enough to make a firm but pliable dough.

3. Knead the dough on a lightly floured surface for 5 minutes. Allow it to rest for 5 minutes. Then add the flaxseed, cracked wheat, bran, and salt.

4. Knead the dough for an additional 20 minutes. Place the dough in a bowl, cover it with a damp cloth, and allow it to rise in a warm spot until almost doubled in bulk, about 3 hours (5 to 6 hours in a cooler location).

5. Turn the dough over once, stretching and deflating it. Cover it, and let it rise again until doubled in bulk, about 2 hours.

6. Punch the dough down. Divide it into 2 equal pieces and form each piece into a loaf. Sprinkle a baking sheet with cornmeal and place the loaves on it. Cover and allow the loaves to rise for 20 minutes. Meanwhile, preheat the oven to 500° F.

7. Brush the tops of the loaves with water and evenly sprinkle cornmeal over them. Slash the top of each loaf once or twice with a sharp knife, and immediately place the loaves in the oven. Toss ½ cup water onto the bottom of the oven to create steam, and bake for 10 minutes. Reduce the heat to 380° F, and bake until the loaves are golden brown with a hard crust, about 35 minutes longer.

Rosemary Ciabatta

For the pre-ferment

¼ cup rye flour

¼ cup stone-ground whole
wheat flour

¼ cup stone-ground white
flour

¼ teaspoon active dry yeast

For the dough

1 tablespoon active dry yeast

4 cups stone-ground white
flour, or unbleached
all-purpose flour

1½ tablespoons salt

3 tablespoons chopped fresh
rosemary, plus 10 whole
small sprigs

Olive oil

MAKES 2 LOAVES

A fantastic, chewy texture and the enticing aroma of fresh rosemary make this bread distinct. Using a "pre-ferment" is a simple technique that adds depth and body to this bread's flavor and texture. It can be used for almost any bread, and only requires a little bit of advance planning: you make a small amount of dough the day before finishing the loaf. This small ball of dough has had a long time to ferment, which allows the yeast to gain strength and results in a savory final product.

Make the pre-ferment

1. Mix the rye flour, whole wheat flour, and white flour together in a small mixing bowl.

2. Stir the yeast into ½ cup warm water until it dissolves.

3. Add ½ teaspoon of the yeast mixture to the flour mixture (discard the remainder of the yeast). Stir in just enough cold water to form a very dry dough, about ¼ cup.

4. Cover the bowl tightly with plastic wrap and set it aside overnight at room temperature.

Prepare the dough and bake the bread

5. Mix the pre-ferment with the yeast and ½ cup warm water in a large mixing bowl. Add the stone-ground white flour and stir in enough warm water to form a wet, sticky dough, 1⅓ to 1½ cups. Knead the dough with a wooden spoon until it becomes elastic, about 5 minutes. Allow the dough to rest for 5 minutes.

6. Add the salt and the chopped rosemary, and knead with the wooden spoon for another 5 minutes. Cover the bowl with a cloth and set it aside at room temperature until the dough has doubled in bulk, about 4 hours in a warm place.

7. Stir the dough a few times to deflate it. Cover the bowl with a cloth and set it aside until the dough has doubled in bulk again, about 2 hours.

8. Preheat the oven to 425° F. Cover a baking sheet with parchment paper, and liberally coat the paper with olive oil.

9. Place the dough on the parchment paper, and form it into a flat, round-edged, rectangular loaf (ciabatta is traditionally said to be shaped like a shoe). Allow it to rise for 15 to 20 minutes.

10. Make dimples in the dough with your fingertips. Spread olive oil over the top, and decorate it with the rosemary sprigs. Bake for 5 minutes. Reduce the heat to 395° and bake for another 25 minutes. The loaf is done when it is brown on top.

Green Olive Round

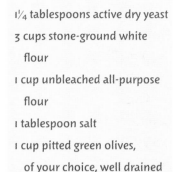

1¼ tablespoons active dry yeast

3 cups stone-ground white
    flour

1 cup unbleached all-purpose
    flour

1 tablespoon salt

1 cup pitted green olives,
    of your choice, well drained

Cornmeal

This recipe was inspired by a sumptuous, pretty, green-olive loaf we once found at a wonderful bakery on the Campo dei Fiori in Rome. At the Lodge, we use a stone-ground "whole white" flour from New Brunswick, but you can substitute any high-quality stone-ground flour.

1. Stir the yeast into ½ cup warm water in a small mixing bowl until it dissolves.

2. In a large mixing bowl, blend the two flours together. Add the yeast mixture and about 2 cups warm water, enough to form a supple dough. Knead the dough on a lightly floured surface for 10 minutes. Allow it to rest for 10 minutes.

3. Add the salt and knead for another 10 minutes. Incorporate the olives, pressing them into the dough.

4. Form the dough into a ball, place in a large bowl, cover, and allow it to rise in a warm spot until almost doubled in bulk, about 3 hours.

5. Punch the dough down to deflate it, and cover and allow it to rise until doubled in bulk again, about 2 hours.

6. Form the dough into a loaf and place it on a baking sheet dusted with cornmeal, or place it in a greased loaf pan, preferably nonstick. Allow it to rise for 20 minutes.

7. Meanwhile, preheat the oven to 380° F.

8. Bake the loaf until a golden crust has formed, about 40 minutes. Remove from the pan and cool on a wire rack.

Sun-Dried-Tomato Bread with White Cornmeal

1 tablespoon active dry yeast

4 cups unbleached all-purpose flour

½ cup stone-ground white cornmeal, yellow cornmeal, or grits

2 teaspoons salt

2 large eggs, beaten

2 tablespoons olive oil

10 sun-dried tomatoes, cut into quarters or large pieces

2 tablespoons coarsely ground or cracked black pepper, optional

We use stone-ground white cornmeal from the New Hope Mill in upstate New York, but you can substitute a high-quality yellow cornmeal. This recipe produces a very light "white" bread, studded with red tomato— delicious toasted for sandwiches.

1. Stir the yeast into ½ cup warm water in a small bowl until dissolved.

2. In a medium mixing bowl, or in the bowl of an electric mixer fitted with the dough hook, blend together the flour and cornmeal. Add the yeast mixture, salt, eggs, and olive oil.

3. While mixing, add about 1 cup warm water, or enough to form a soft but not sticky dough. Add the sun-dried tomatoes and the optional pepper. Knead on a lightly floured surface for 20 minutes.

4. Cover the bowl with a clean towel and set it aside until the dough has doubled in bulk, about 4 hours.

5. Punch the dough down to deflate it, and set it aside again until doubled in bulk, about 7 hours.

6. Meanwhile, preheat the oven to 385° F. Grease two loaf pans (preferably nonstick) with olive oil.

7. Divide the dough in half and place the portions in the prepared loaf pans. Bake until the loaves rise and turn golden on top, about 40 minutes. Remove the loaves from the pans and allow to cool on a wire rack before cutting.

Herb Garden Bread

1½ tablespoons active dry yeast

5 cups unbleached all-purpose flour

1¼ cups extra virgin olive oil, plus extra for the baking sheet

1 tablespoon chopped fresh thyme or lemon thyme

1 teaspoon coarsely chopped rosemary

¼ cup chopped fresh sage leaves

1½ tablespoons chopped fresh oregano

6 garlic cloves, coarsely chopped

1 tablespoon freshly cracked black pepper

¾ cup whole milk

1 cup coarse yellow cornmeal, plus extra for dusting the loaf

2 tablespoons salt, plus extra for sprinkling on the loaf

We make this bread, loosely based on Italian focaccia, in the summer and fall, when the Lodge's herb garden overflows with thyme, oregano, rosemary, and beautiful sage. The two secrets to making this bread are to keep the dough moist—it should be too sticky to knead with your hands, but not so wet it won't stay together—and to use generous quantities of olive oil. The bread should bathe in olive oil while baking.

1. Stir the yeast into ½ cup warm water in a large mixing bowl until dissolved. Add 1 cup of the flour and blend it in. Set the mixture aside.

2. Heat ¾ cup of the olive oil in a medium skillet over medium-high heat. Add the chopped herbs, the garlic, and the pepper, and sauté until fragrant, 1 to 2 minutes. Add the milk and remove the skillet from the heat.

3. Add the remaining 4 cups flour and the cornmeal to the mixing bowl containing the yeast mixture. Pour the hot herb mixture over the flour. Add about 2 cups warm water, enough to form a very wet, sticky dough. Knead the dough with a wooden spoon or spatula for 5 minutes.

4. Let the dough rest for 5 minutes. Add the salt.

5. Knead the dough for another 8 minutes, or until it forms a consistent, elastic mass.

6. Cover and allow the dough to rise in a warm spot until doubled in bulk, 2 to 3 hours.

7. Flip the dough over in the bowl, and allow it to rise until doubled in bulk again, about 1½ hours.

8. Preheat the oven to 425° F. Cover a baking sheet with parchment paper, and coat the parchment with olive oil.

9. Spread the dough onto the baking sheet and allow it to rise for 20 minutes.

10. Using your fingertips, make dimples in the top of the bread. Pour the remaining ½ cup olive oil over the top, and dust the top with cornmeal and a little salt. Toss ½ cup water onto the bottom of the oven to create steam. Bake for 10 minutes.

11. Lower the oven temperature to 400° and bake until the top of the loaf has turned golden, about 30 minutes. Remove the loaf from the pan and cool on a wire rack for at least 20 minutes before cutting.

Chapter seven

Desserts

There are lots of Strawberries and Raspberries in certain places [and] some little blue and red fruits in the woods. I have seen small delicate pears; and in the fields all winter there are certain little fruits like little apples colored red, from which we make cotignac for dessert. There are lots of currants that look like ours [in France], but they tend towards red; some of these other currants are round ones we call Guedres.

—Marc Lescarbot, *Histoire de la Nouvelle-France,* 1609

As Monsieur Lescarbot noted more than 390 years ago, Trout Point has the great fortune of having an abundance of wild fruits suited for sumptuous desserts, including strawberries, raspberries, blueberries, serviceberries, blackberries, and currants. As for other fruits like the "delicate pears" Lescarbot mentions, we can only wonder about their identity. We take advantage of seasonal fruits, always keeping in mind how good they are when combined with sweets like French-style pâtisserie and chocolate, desserts that Lescarbot and his companions initiated on Nova Scotia soil. ("Cotignac" is a method of baking and seasoning fruit, usually quince, to use for desserts.) In the summer we make ice creams, and in the fall, warm Chocolate Gourmandise. Varieties of delicious bread puddings, studded with fruit, white chocolate, and nuts, find their way regularly onto the Trout Point dessert menu as well.

Basic Short Dough for Pie and Tart Crusts

1¾ cups sugar

3½ cups (7 sticks) unsalted
  butter, cut into small pieces

2 eggs

2 teaspoons pure vanilla
  extract

8½ cups all-purpose flour

We use this short dough crust for a variety of tarts. The recipe makes a large batch; you can store the dough tightly sealed in the refrigerator for up to 2 weeks or in the freezer for up to a month.

1. Combine the sugar, butter, eggs, and vanilla in a large bowl and mix with a whisk or with an electric mixer on low speed. Mix until the ingredients are just combined; do not overwork.

2. With vigorous whisking motions or on medium speed, add the flour a bit at a time, until the mixture is combined and smooth (small chunks of butter may remain). Do not overmix, or the dough will become tough and mealy. Stop mixing as soon as the dough forms a cohesive mass and can be formed into a ball.

3. Using a scale, divide the dough into 7 equal parts. Shape each one into a ball, wrap it tightly in plastic wrap, and refrigerate. The dough can be stored in the refrigerator for up to 2 weeks or in the freezer for up to 1 month (thaw in refrigerator before rolling out).

4. When you are ready to use the dough, remove the plastic wrap and place the dough on a floured work surface. Press on the ball to form a 1½-inch-thick disk. Roll it out according to the instructions in the pie or tart recipe.

Using the Basic Short Dough

You can use this crust for all sorts of pies and crusts—not just the ones in this book.

If you're making a pie or tart that calls for a prebaked crust, fit the rolled-out crust into the pie pan; then line the crust with parchment paper and fill it with pie weights or dried beans. Bake it in a preheated 375° F oven for 10 to 15 minutes. Then remove the parchment and the weights, and fill as called for in the recipe.

If you will be filling the crust and then baking the pie, fit the rolled-out crust into the pie pan and chill it in the freezer for 15 minutes before filling it. This will allow the crust to bake without softening too much. Then fill and bake according to the recipe instructions.

Wild Blackberry Custard Tart

SERVES 8

1 Basic Short Dough crust
(page 180)
4 cups fresh blackberries
5 tablespoons pure maple
syrup
1 tablespoon balsamic vinegar
¾ cup sugar
2 eggs
2 egg yolks
1¼ cups heavy cream
1 teaspoon pure vanilla extract

Wild blackberry bushes line the road to the Great Lodge. We pick bowlfuls in August, to the delight of our guests. Here is one of our favorite recipes for this delectable fruit. We use the taller-sided springform pan to achieve slightly higher and more irregular, rustic sides on the tart. You can also use a regular tart pan with a removable bottom.

1. Roll out the dough on a lightly floured surface, forming a 12-inch round. Line a 10-inch springform or tart pan with a removable bottom with the dough and place it in the freezer.

2. Stir the blackberries, maple syrup, vinegar, and ½ cup of the sugar together in a medium bowl. Allow this mixture to macerate for at least 30 minutes.

3. Preheat the oven to 385° F.

4. In a small mixing bowl, whisk together the eggs, egg yolks, cream, vanilla, and the remaining ¼ cup sugar. Blend well but do not beat.

5. Spread the blackberry mixture evenly in the chilled tart shell. Pour the custard mixture over the berries.

6. Bake until the custard turns golden, about 40 minutes. Allow the tart to cool on a wire rack for at least 40 minutes. Remove the sides of the pan, and serve.

To Macerate

In culinary terms, to macerate a fruit means to soak it in a liquid so that it absorbs that liquid's flavor and also softens somewhat, changing its texture. Alcohols, liqueurs, and vinegars are commonly used for maceration. By contrast, one *marinates* meats or vegetables, with similar goals.

Trout Point Cheesecake

SERVES 16

8 eggs

⅞ cup sugar

Three 8-ounce packages cream cheese, room temperature

1 Basic Short Dough crust (page 180)

Blackberry or other fruit jam

Fresh fruit for garnish

1. Preheat the oven to 325° F.
2. Using a whisk or an electric mixer, blend the eggs, sugar, and cream cheese in a large mixing bowl until thoroughly mixed and creamy.
3. Roll out the dough on a lightly floured surface, forming a 9-inch round. Line the bottom (not the sides) of a springform cake pan with the crust, and freeze the crust for 15 minutes. Pour the cream cheese mixture into the chilled crust.
4. Bake until the filling has solidified and is beginning to expand in volume, 35 to 40 minutes. Allow the cheesecake to cool on a wire rack. Remove the sides of the pan. Then transfer it to the refrigerator to chill thoroughly.
5. Top the cheesecake with jam, garnish with fresh fruit, and serve.

Chocolate Cherry Cheesecake

Soak ½ cup dried sour cherries in ½ cup light rum for 1 hour. Melt 7 ounces unsweetened chocolate in the microwave or in a double boiler, and allow it to cool slightly. Prepare the cream cheese mixture for the Trout Point cheesecake, substituting 1 heaping cup sugar for the ⅞ cup and stirring in the melted chocolate. Pour the mixture into the springform pan, and then drop in the drained macerated cherries. Bake as directed.

Pineapple Mint Chocolate Mousse

2¼ cups sugar

40 fresh pineapple mint (or
   other variety of mint) leaves,
   plus extra leaves for garnish

6 ounces semisweet chocolate

2 ounces bittersweet chocolate

4 ounces unsweetened
   chocolate

12 tablespoons (1½ sticks)
   unsalted butter

5 eggs, separated

1 cup heavy cream

This rich, dark chocolate mousse is complemented by homemade pineapple mint syrup. If possible, use mint leaves still attached to their stems. The stems lend substantial flavor to the syrup, and it saves having to pick off the leaves.

1. Combine 2 cups of the sugar with 2 cups water in a saucepan and bring to a boil over medium-high heat. Reduce the heat to low and add half of the pineapple mint leaves (including the stems, if you have them). Simmer until reduced by half, about 20 minutes. Add the remaining mint leaves and simmer for another 5 minutes. Strain the syrup into a bowl and set it aside.

2. Combine the three chocolates and the butter in the top of a double boiler, and heat, stirring frequently, over medium-low heat, until melted. Remove from the heat.

3. In a medium mixing bowl, gently beat the egg yolks. Add a little bit of the hot chocolate mixture and stir well. Then gradually mix in the remaining chocolate and ¾ cup of the pineapple mint syrup, blending thoroughly.

4. Whip the cream in a mixing bowl until soft peaks form. Set it aside.

5. In another mixing bowl, whip the egg whites with an electric mixer until they form soft peaks. Add the remaining ¼ cup sugar, and whip until they form stiff, but not dry, peaks.

6. Gently fold one-fourth of the chocolate mixture into the egg whites. Then gradually add the remainder. Mix in the whipped cream.

7. Pour the mousse into martini or margarita glasses and refrigerate for at least 1 hour.

8. Garnish the mousse with mint leaves, and if desired, drizzle with leftover pineapple mint syrup. Serve.

Flourless Chocolate Almond Cake with White and Dark Chocolate Ganache

For the cake

2 cups ground blanched almonds

1½ cups confectioners' sugar

⅔ cup unsweetened cocoa powder

12 large egg whites

¼ cup granulated sugar

For the dark chocolate ganache

½ cup heavy cream mixed with ½ cup water

1 pound bittersweet chocolate

7 tablespoons unsalted butter

For the white chocolate ganache

1½ pounds white chocolate

1½ cups heavy cream

2 tablespoons unsalted butter

This elegant, rich cake serves perfectly for special occasions—it is our standard dessert for guests' birthdays at the Lodge. It is also simple to make and assemble; the only secrets are to whip the egg whites until they form peaks that are stiff but not dry, and to very gently fold in the dry ingredients before pouring the batter into the cake pans. This delicate cake can be prone to burning, so keep a careful eye on it while it is baking, turning the pans as necessary if your oven tends to be hotter on one side than the other.

Prepare the cake

1. Preheat the oven to 375° F.

2. Butter two 9-inch round cake pans.

3. In a large mixing bowl, whisk together the ground almonds, confectioners' sugar, and cocoa powder, ensuring that there are no lumps.

4. Whip the egg whites in a large bowl until they start to form soft peaks. Add the granulated sugar, and whip until stiff peaks form.

5. Using a rubber spatula, add a small amount of the dry ingredients to the egg whites. Then add more, a little at a time, until the mixture has turned chocolate-colored and all the dry ingredients are completely incorporated.

6. Pour half of this mixture into each prepared cake pan, and bake for about 15 minutes, or until the center is firm and springs back when touched.

7. Remove the cakes from the pans, and allow them to cool on a wire rack for 10 minutes. Then either refrigerate or proceed immediately to the assembly of the cake.

Prepare the dark chocolate ganache

8. Heat the cream mixture in a large saucepan over medium heat until it reaches the simmering point. Then reduce the heat to low and add the chocolate. Stir frequently until it has melted into the cream. Remove the pan from the heat and allow the mixture to cool for about 10 minutes.

9. Cut the butter into slices, and stir them, one or two pieces at a time, into the chocolate mixture. Refrigerate until thickened, about 1 hour. (Both the dark and white chocolate ganaches can be made in advance and kept in the refrigerator for up to 2 days. Let them warm at room temperature, whisking occasionally, until they're a spreadable consistency.)

Prepare the white chocolate ganache

10. Put the white chocolate in a heatproof bowl that is large enough to hold the cream.

11. Combine the cream and the butter in a medium saucepan over medium heat, and bring the mixture to a boil. Immediately remove the pan from the heat and pour the hot cream over the white chocolate. Allow the chocolate to heat for 2 minutes. Then stir gently until the mixture is smooth and creamy. Refrigerate until thickened, about 1 hour.

For the final assembly

12. Place one of the cake layers on a serving plate, top side up. Using a rubber spatula, spread the white chocolate ganache over the layer. Place the second layer on top, bottom side up. Cover the top and sides of the cake with the dark chocolate ganache. Refrigerate the cake for at least 2 hours before serving.

Blueberry Bread Pudding

1 loaf day-old French bread, preferably a good-quality baguette, broken into large pieces

1 quart whole milk, or more as needed

4 tablespoons (½ stick) unsalted butter

3 large eggs

1½ cups sugar

2 tablespoons pure vanilla extract

Wild blueberry–macadamia nut filling

2 cups fresh blueberries, preferably the wild variety

1 cup coarsely chopped macadamia nuts

Nothing completes a Creole meal better than a bread pudding brimming with the flavors of fruits, nuts, and vanilla. We've made more than twenty variations on the classic bread pudding, using whatever is fresh and available. You'll find three variations following the main recipe, but feel free to experiment with whatever seasonal ingredients appeal to you. Try to leave the mixture fairly lumpy—it shouldn't resemble a paste. This recipe produces a firm, sliceable loaf.

1. In a large mixing bowl, soak the bread pieces in the milk until they are soggy but not falling apart, 20 to 30 minutes.

2. Meanwhile, preheat the oven to 350° F. Heavily grease a loaf pan with the butter.

3. Add the eggs, sugar, and vanilla to the bread and milk, and mix thoroughly.

4. Stir in the blueberries and nuts, and pour the mixture into the prepared loaf pan.

5. Bake for 45 minutes, or until the pudding has risen and the top has turned golden brown. Remove the pan from the oven and allow the pudding to cool for at least 20 minutes before serving.

Bread Pudding Variations

Substitute any of the following combinations for the blueberries and macadamia nuts in the Blueberry Bread Pudding.

Plum, Walnut, and White Chocolate

5 purple or other dark plums,
    pitted and cut into wedges
¾ cup whole walnuts
4 ounces white chocolate,
    broken into large chunks

Rum Raisin

1½ cups sultana (golden)
    raisins
½ cup dark rum

In a small, wide bowl, soak the raisins in the rum for at least 1 hour; then add to the pudding mixture.

Dried Cherry, White Chocolate, and Almond

½ cup (packed) dried sour
    cherries
4 ounces white chocolate,
    broken into large chunks
½ cup slivered blanched
    almonds

Peach Tart with Lemon-Almond Cream

SERVES 8

4 to 5 medium peaches, pitted
and quartered

¾ cup granulated sugar

1 Basic Short Dough crust
(page 180)

8 tablespoons (1 stick)
unsalted butter, room
temperature

½ cup confectioners' sugar

½ teaspoon baking powder

1 egg, lightly beaten

1 cup unbleached all-purpose
flour

1 cup ground toasted blanched
almonds (see page 23)

Zest of ½ lemon

1 tablespoon fresh lemon juice

The combination of fresh peaches, toasted almonds, and a hint of tart, savory lemon makes this beautiful dessert the ultimate culmination of a summer meal. The thick lemon-almond cream can be combined with other fruit as well, such as plums or apricots.

1. Preheat the oven to 375° F.

2. Mix the peach slices and granulated sugar together in a mixing bowl. Set aside.

3. Roll the dough out on a lightly floured surface, forming an 11-inch round. Fit the crust into a 9-inch tart pan with a removable bottom. Cover the crust with parchment paper and weight it down with pie weights.

4. Bake the crust for 15 minutes, or until the edges start to brown. Remove it from the oven, and remove the parchment and the weights.

5. In a medium mixing bowl or in a food processor, blend together the butter, confectioners' sugar, baking powder, and egg. Slowly incorporate the flour and ground almonds. Mix in the lemon zest and juice.

6. Spread the almond cream evenly over the bottom of the tart crust. Arrange the peach slices evenly around the tart, pressing each slice into the cream.

7. Bake for approximately 35 minutes, until the cream starts to turn golden. Remove the sides of the pan. Serve hot or at room temperature.

Apricot Tart

1 Basic Short Dough crust
  (page 180)
10 to 12 ripe fresh apricots,
  halved and pitted
½ cup sugar
¼ cup Cointreau

"The best apricot dessert I've ever had!" many Trout Point guests have exclaimed after finishing this extremely simple but stupendously flavorful tart. One key is to use *ripe* apricots. Another is the combination of the orange-flavored Cointreau with the apricots, which makes for a flawless complement of tastes. For a variation, line five or six individual tart pans with the dough and filling, and bake them for about 10 minutes. Sliced fresh peaches can be substituted for the apricots as in the photograph to the right.

1. Roll the dough out on a lightly floured surface, forming a 10-inch round. Fit the round into an 8-inch tart pan, and chill it in the freezer until ready to bake.

2. In a medium mixing bowl, toss the apricot halves with the sugar and Cointreau. Set aside for 1 to 3 hours, allowing the apricots to soften and the flavors and juices to blend together.

3. Preheat the oven to 400° F.

4. Arrange the apricot halves in concentric circles inside the chilled tart shell, placing them as close together as possible. (The apricots will shrink during cooking, and you do not want to have large areas of crust exposed.) Pour the remaining Cointreau/apricot syrup over the apricot halves.

5. Bake for 10 minutes. Then reduce the heat to 385° and bake until the crust is golden brown and the tops of the apricots are beginning to brown, about 25 minutes. Let the tart cool on a wire rack for 20 minutes before serving.

Blueberry Tart

2 pints fresh wild blueberries

5 tablespoons pure maple
syrup

¾ cup sugar

2 tablespoons unbleached all-
purpose flour

1 tablespoon balsamic vinegar

1 Basic Short Dough crust
(page 180)

Marc Lescarbot would have liked this tart, since it combines the French predilection for delicate fruit tarts with wild blueberries and real Canadian maple syrup, representing the bountiful wild foods found in Nova Scotia, *la nouvelle France*.

1. Combine the blueberries, maple syrup, sugar, flour, and balsamic vinegar in a medium glass or stainless steel mixing bowl, and set aside for about 1 hour.

2. Roll the dough out on a lightly floured surface, forming a 10-inch round. Place the dough in an 8-inch tart pan with a removable bottom, and chill it in the freezer for 30 minutes.

3. Preheat the oven to 400° F. Position a rack in the center of the oven.

4. Pour the filling into the frozen tart shell and immediately place it in the oven, on the middle rack. Bake for 10 minutes. Then reduce the heat to 375° and bake for approximately 35 minutes, until the crust is golden and crumbly. The individual berries should still be distinguishable in the filling.

5. Allow the tart to cool for 20 minutes. Remove the sides of the tart pan and serve.

Apple Tart

1 Basic Short Dough crust
(page 180)

3 large or 4 medium tart
apples, such as Granny Smith
or Cortland

4 tablespoons (½ stick) chilled
unsalted butter, cut into
small pieces

A hint of almond extract adds an extra dimension to this tart, which can be prepared in less than an hour.

1. Roll the dough out on a lightly floured surface, forming an 11-inch round. Fit the dough into a 9-inch tart pan, and chill it in the freezer for 30 minutes.

½ cup plus 2 tablespoons
  sugar
1 teaspoon pure almond
  extract

2. While the crust is chilling, preheat the oven to 385° F.

3. Peel and quarter the apples. Cut the quarters into slices that are ¼ inch thick at the outer edge.

4. Toss the apple slices, butter, and sugar together in a mixing bowl.

5. Place a large skillet over medium heat, add the apple mixture, and sauté until the apples just start to soften and sweat, about 5 minutes. Remove the pan from the heat and stir in the almond extract.

6. Arrange the apple slices decoratively in the chilled tart shell, pour the cooking juices over the apples, and bake until the crust is golden, about 40 minutes.

Peach Custard Tart

5 large, firm peaches, pitted,
  and cut into wedges

5 tablespoons Cointreau or
  Triple Sec

¾ cup granulated sugar

1½ cups unbleached
  all-purpose flour

½ cup ground blanched
  almonds

⅔ cup confectioners' sugar

11 tablespoons chilled unsalted
  butter, cut into small pieces,
  plus extra for the cake pan

4 eggs

1 cup heavy cream

1 teaspoon pure almond
  extract

You can substitute another fruit for the peaches in this elegant dish—we like a combination of rhubarb and strawberries. Whatever fruit you use, this tart will impress your guests with its beauty and luscious flavor.

1. In a medium mixing bowl, toss the peaches with the Cointreau and ½ cup of the granulated sugar. Allow this mixture to sit for at least 1 hour to macerate.

2. Heat the peach mixture in a medium skillet over medium heat. Cook until the peaches start to soften, approximately 10 minutes (depending on their ripeness). Remove from the heat and set aside.

3. Preheat the oven to 375° F.

4. In a medium mixing bowl, blend together ½ cup of the flour, the almonds, and the confectioners' sugar.

5. Using your hands, mix in 8 tablespoons of the butter. When you have a consistent dough, beat 1 egg and add it to the dough. Incorporate the remaining 1 cup flour little by little.

6. Form the dough into a ball, and roll it out on a lightly floured surface, forming an 11-inch round.

7. Butter the bottom and sides of a 9-inch springform pan and fit the dough into the pan. The dough should come up to a height of 1½ to 1¾ inches on the sides of the pan. Cover the crust with parchment paper and weight it down with pie weights or dried beans.

8. Bake the crust until the edges turn brown, about 20 minutes. Remove the pan from the oven and set it aside.

9. Melt the remaining 3 tablespoons butter in a small pan over low heat. Set it aside.

10. In a mixing bowl, gently whisk together the cream, remaining 3 eggs, almond extract, melted butter, remaining granulated sugar, and any excess liquid from the peaches. Blend but do not whip.

11. Arrange the peaches evenly in the tart crust, and pour the custard mixture over them. Bake until the custard has risen, set, and started to turn golden, about 40 minutes.

12. Remove the pan from the oven and allow the tart to cool for at least 20 minutes before removing the sides of the pan and serving. It may be served warm or at room temperature.

Wild Blackberry Curd Tart

1 Basic Short Dough crust
  (page 180)

4 cups fresh blackberries

¼ cup confectioners' sugar

2 teaspoons grated lemon zest

2 teaspoons balsamic vinegar

2 eggs

3 egg yolks

1 cup granulated sugar

8 tablespoons (1 stick)
  unsalted butter, cut into
  8 pieces

Ronnie Harris—who helped build the Great Lodge by assisting the stonemasons and who now works everywhere and anywhere we need him—loves to pick wild blackberries so we can make a fresh tart, some of which he will inevitably sample before it goes out to the guests. One day we invented this blackberry curd, which requires milling the blackberries through a *passetout*, or food mill. Upon seeing all the milled seeds and skins, Ronnie exclaimed that he would never pick blackberries again if we were "just going to waste them." When he tasted this tart, however, he quickly changed his mind and requested another helping. It's now one of our (and Ronnie's) favorites when wild blackberries are in season.

1. Preheat the oven to 375° F.

2. Roll out the dough on a lightly floured surface, forming an 11-inch round. Fit the crust into a 9-inch tart pan with a removable bottom. Line the crust with parchment paper and weight it down with pie weights.

3. Bake the crust for 15 minutes, or until the edges start to brown. Remove it from the oven, and remove the parchment and weights. Set the crust aside to cool.

4. In a medium mixing bowl, gently toss together 2 cups of the blackberries, the confectioners' sugar, lemon zest, and vinegar. Set aside.

5. Place the remaining 2 cups of blackberries in a food mill and process. Reserve ½ cup plus 2 tablespoons of the processed juice and discard the seeds and skins.

6. Combine the eggs, yolks, and granulated sugar in a double boiler over medium-low heat. Stir frequently until the mixture thickens enough to coat the back of a spoon, about 8 minutes.

7. Slowly stir the butter, one piece at a time, into the mixture in the double boiler.

8. When all the butter has blended into the mixture, add the reserved blackberry juice, stirring constantly. Keep stirring until a few bubbles start to appear in the curd and it has thickened substantially, 8 to 10 minutes. Remove the pan from the heat.

9. Pour the curd mixture into the tart shell. Spread the mixture of whole blackberries evenly over the tart, on top of the curd. Allow to cool for at least 2 hours before removing the sides of the pan and serving. The tart can be refrigerated for up to 2 days.

Chocolate Gourmandise

4 ounces bittersweet chocolate

2 ounces semisweet or milk chocolate

1 cup (2 sticks) unsalted butter

11 large marshmallows

6 eggs, chilled

1½ cups sugar

½ cup unbleached all-purpose flour

We must thank fellow cookbook author and food critic Patricia Wells for the basic concept behind this recipe, which has been a favorite among Trout Point guests for years. It's important to work with cold eggs just out of the refrigerator, and to not let the final mixture heat up to room temperature before baking; otherwise the dessert will not rise properly. Try topping this with Wintergreen Crème Anglaise (page 83) before serving.

1. Combine the two chocolates and the butter in a double boiler over medium heat. Stir frequently until just before the butter has fully melted. Remove the pan from the heat and stir until the butter is thoroughly combined with the chocolate. Set it aside.

2. Preheat the oven to 390° F. Butter and flour eleven ramekins. Put a marshmallow in each ramekin.

3. In a medium mixing bowl, preferably one with a spout to make pouring easier, combine the eggs, sugar, and flour. Do not beat or whip the egg mixture, as this will affect the texture of the finished dessert. Instead, gently blend the ingredients together until thoroughly mixed.

4. Fold the chocolate mixture into the egg mixture, stirring until completely blended. Pour this evenly into the ramekins, over the marshmallows. Bake for about 17 minutes, or until the sides are thoroughly cooked and the center is still liquid.

5. Serve warm or cold, either in the ramekins or turned out onto a plate.

Wine-Poached Pears

1 bottle dry red wine

2 cups sugar

1 pinch mace

1 whole clove

One 3-inch cinnamon stick

4 firm-fleshed, not overly ripe
pears, such as D'Anjou or
Bartlett, peeled and cored,
left whole

1. Combine the wine, sugar, mace, clove, and cinnamon stick in a large saucepan, and bring to a simmer over medium heat. Add the pears and poach gently until tender, 15 to 20 minutes. Using a slotted spoon, transfer the pears to individual dessert bowls.

2. Cook the wine mixture over medium heat until reduced by half, about 20 minutes. Strain the wine, pour it over the pears, and serve.

Maple Crème Brûlée

1 quart heavy cream

4 eggs

8 egg yolks

¾ cup packed light brown sugar

½ cup plus 2 tablespoons pure maple syrup

1 tablespoon pure vanilla extract

¼ cup grated maple sugar or lightly packed dark brown sugar

We've taken the Creole crème brûlée—a New Orleans classic—and added pure maple syrup for a little Canadian twist.

1. Preheat the oven to 350° F.

2. Heat the cream in a medium saucepan over medium heat, stirring frequently, until it reaches the simmering point.

3. While the cream is warming, combine the eggs, yolks, light brown sugar, maple syrup, and vanilla in a large mixing bowl and blend together—but do not beat or whip.

4. Pour a small amount of the hot cream into the egg mixture, stirring constantly. Slowly add the remaining cream, incorporating it thoroughly.

5. Place ten ramekins in a baking dish, and pour warm water into the dish to reach halfway up the sides of the ramekins.

6. Pour the cream mixture evenly into the ramekins, and place the baking dish in the oven. Bake until the custard is set, 30 to 40 minutes. Remove the dish from the oven and remove the ramekins from the water bath.

7. Cover each ramekin with plastic wrap, and refrigerate for at least 2 hours. (The crème brûlée can be stored like this for up to 1 week.)

8. Just before serving, preheat the broiler.

9. Evenly coat the top of each dessert with a thin layer of maple sugar. Place the ramekins under the broiler until the sugar has boiled and thoroughly caramelized, 1 minute. (You can also use a chef's propane torch to caramelize the sugar.) Serve immediately.

Lemongrass Crème Brûlée

1 quart heavy cream

5 fresh lemongrass stalks,
coarsely chopped and
crushed

3 Kaffir lime leaves, or
3 teaspoons grated lime
zest

4 eggs

8 egg yolks

½ cup granulated sugar

2 tablespoons pure maple
syrup

½ teaspoon pure vanilla
extract

¼ cup lightly packed dark
brown sugar

Here's another crème brûlée variation. The subtle citrus flavors of lemongrass and lime leaves add enough sweetness on their own, so we've reduced the sugar and added a touch of maple syrup instead.

1. Preheat the oven to 350° F.

2. Pour the cream into a medium saucepan, and add the lemongrass and the lime leaves. Place over medium heat and stir frequently until the cream reaches the simmering point.

3. While the cream is warming, combine the eggs, yolks, granulated sugar, maple syrup, and vanilla in a large mixing bowl and blend together—but do not beat or whip.

4. Strain the hot cream. Pour a small amount into the egg mixture, stirring constantly. Then slowly add more of the cream until it is all incorporated.

5. Place ten ramekins in a baking dish, and pour warm water into the dish to reach halfway up the sides of the ramekins.

6. Pour the cream mixture evenly into the ramekins, and place the baking dish in the oven. Bake until the custard is set, 30 to 40 minutes. Remove the dish from the oven and remove the ramekins from the water bath.

7. Cover the top of each ramekin with plastic wrap, and refrigerate for at least 2 hours. (The crème brûlée can be stored like this for up to 1 week.)

8. Just before serving, preheat the broiler.

9. Evenly coat the top of each dessert with a thin layer of dark brown sugar. Place the ramekins under the broiler until the sugar has boiled and thoroughly caramelized, 1 minute. (You can also use a chef's propane torch to caramelize the sugar.) Serve immediately.

Maple Ice Cream

1 pound maple sugar, grated

12 egg yolks

10 cups heavy cream

¾ cup pure maple syrup

The natural anti-freezing properties of the maple syrup in this recipe help to keep the ice cream soft and creamy.

1. Fill a large bowl halfway with ice, and set it aside.

2. Place the maple sugar and egg yolks in a large mixing bowl. Beat together until the mixture is well blended and has taken on a lemony color.

3. In a large saucepan, bring the cream to a simmer over medium heat. Do not burn the cream. Add the maple syrup. Remove the pan from the heat.

4. Add a small amount of the hot cream to the egg yolk mixture, stirring constantly. Slowly add the remaining cream, stirring until it is thoroughly blended. Put the mixing bowl in the bowl of ice, and stir until chilled.

5. Put the mixture in an ice-cream maker, and process according to the manufacturer's directions. Freeze until ready to serve.

Coconut Ice Cream

MAKES 2 QUARTS

12 egg yolks

1½ cups granulated sugar

5 cups heavy cream

5 cups whole coconut milk

½ cup grated maple sugar

½ cup vodka

1. Fill a large bowl halfway with ice, and set it aside.

2. Combine the egg yolks and granulated sugar in a large mixing bowl. Beat together until the mixture is well blended and lemon-colored.

3. Combine the cream with the coconut milk in a large saucepan, and bring to a simmer over medium heat. Do not let the mixture burn. Remove the pan from the heat.

4. Add a small amount of the hot cream mixture to the egg yolk mixture, stirring constantly. Slowly add the remaining cream, stirring until it is thoroughly blended. Stir in the

maple sugar. Put the mixing bowl in the bowl of ice, and stir until chilled. Then stir in the vodka.

5. Put the mixture in an ice-cream maker, and process according to the manufacturer's directions. Freeze until ready to serve.

White Chocolate–Pistachio Ice Cream

MAKES 2 QUARTS

9 egg yolks

1 cup sugar

5 cups heavy cream

1 cup pure maple syrup

1 cup coarsely chopped white chocolate

1 cup unsalted pistachios, roasted (see page 23)

½ cup Pedro Jiménez wine or other syrupy dessert wine

This is one of the richest and most delicious ice creams we have produced.

1. Fill a large bowl halfway with ice, and set it aside.
2. Combine the egg yolks and sugar in a large mixing bowl. Beat together until the mixture is well blended and lemon-colored.
3. Bring the cream to a simmer in a large saucepan over medium heat. Do not let the cream burn. Add the maple syrup and remove the pan from the heat.
4. Add a small amount of the hot cream to the egg yolk mixture, stirring constantly. Slowly add the remaining cream, stirring until it is thoroughly blended. Stir in the white chocolate, pistachios, and wine. Put the mixing bowl in the bowl of ice, and stir until chilled.
5. Put the mixture in an ice-cream maker, and process according to the manufacturer's directions. Freeze until ready to serve.

Chapter eight

Smoking Seafood

Smoking preserves foods and imparts subtle flavors, while also creating delightfully unique textures in seafood. Nova Scotia is blessed with North America's best summer climate: rainfall, temperature, and humidity are all moderate. At Trout Point we are able to successfully smoke seafood from March into November. There are many smoking methods. We prefer the technique of cold-smoking seafood, using spruce sawdust, as opposed to other types of hard- or softwood. This sawdust produces a light smokiness that doesn't compete with the flavors of the seafood.

The Smokehouse

The smokehouse at Trout Point is a very simple structure that can easily be built in a backyard during a long weekend. The four walls are each about four feet by ten feet, constructed of two-by-fours and wood siding—clapboard in our case—with enough narrow space between the boards to allow air to come in and waft the smoke up and over the seafood. One of the walls has a wooden door (we salvaged a house's interior door). There is a simple metal gable roof. The natural holes and gaps of the board construction and the ridging in the metal roof create enough ventilation to allow the smoke to escape slowly. The floor is coarse gravel, allowing a safe place for the burning sawdust. Shelf brackets hold wire racks (like those used for cooling breads) on which we place the seafood.

When the weather is hot, or the particular seafood is more sensitive to heat, or a lot of smoke is desired, we use an exterior firebox, which is connected to the smokehouse with inexpensive stovepipe. Ours is a fifty-five-gallon drum, closed on both ends, with the side cut out and fashioned into a door. (Anyone with basic welding experience and equipment can do this in short order.) The stovepipe runs from the top of the drum to the bottom of the smokehouse. When the smoke drafts through the stovepipe, it cools, ensuring that the temperature inside the smokehouse never becomes too high.

Preparing for Smoking

The first step in the smoking process is the salting of the seafood. Salting removes excess moisture and increases the salt levels in the fish, both of which give it some protection against microbial contamination until the smoking process is completed.

Rinse the seafood and then pat it dry. Next, place the seafood in a large container and cover it completely with coarse salt, preferably kosher salt. After sufficient salting (as determined by the type of fish), rinse off the salt, and set the seafood to dry on a wire rack until it is barely dry to the touch. Now the seafood is ready to be placed inside the smokehouse.

The Smoking Process

To make the fire, mound a pile of hardwood or spruce sawdust inside the smokehouse or the exterior firebox, and make a well in the center. Place some kindling in the well, and light the kindling and sawdust (we use a propane torch—it lights more reliably and allows some control over the amount of burning sawdust produced). When the flame dies down and the sawdust is smoldering, close the door and let the sawdust smolder for one hour. Then place the seafood in the smokehouse and smoke it.

There should be enough sawdust inside the smokehouse to allow for a continuous smolder for the appropriate amount of time, which varies by recipe. One large feed sack of dry sawdust should burn between eighteen and twenty hours. If you do need to add additional sawdust, add it to the outside, unburned part of the pile. The fire should never be so close to the seafood that the fish or shellfish feels warm to the touch.

In most cases the temperature in the smokehouse should not rise above 96° F nor fall below 50° F. In warmer times, we often find it necessary to burn the sawdust in an external firebox to avoid temperatures above 96° inside the smokehouse. (Temperatures above this level favor bacterial growth and cause a pellicle, or skin, which is impervious to smoke, to form on the seafood.)

Smoked Salmon Fillets

1 large salmon fillet, 8 to 20
   ounces
Coarse salt
Spices and herbs, such as
   freshly ground fennel seed,
   fresh dill leaves, and allspice,
   or cracked black pepper,
   optional
Pure maple syrup, optional

Serve home-smoked salmon with toast and sweet mustard, or with crème fraîche and capers. The freshly smoked salmon will keep for about two weeks in the refrigerator. Toward the end of the two weeks, the smoked salmon is best used for cooking—it can be pan-fried and used in recipes as a substitute for bacon (see recipes such as Smoked Salmon Spaghetti alla Carbonara, page 122).

1. Rinse the salmon fillet and pat it dry. Place the fillet in a single layer in a large, flat container, and cover with the coarse salt. Set aside for 1¾ to 2 hours. (The spices and herbs or cracked black pepper can be rubbed on the fish before or after salting.)

2. Rinse the salt off the fish under cold running water. Set the salmon aside until it is dry to the touch.

3. Meanwhile, light a sawdust pile in the smokehouse at least 1 hour in advance.

4. If using the maple syrup, rub the salmon with it and allow the fish to dry for 10 minutes before smoking. Place the salmon in the smokehouse and smoke for 12 to 36 hours, turning once after 3 hours and then turning every 8 hours until done. If the weather is cool, you can smoke the salmon for as long as 36 hours. The longer the smoking time, the stronger the smoky flavor. We prefer to smoke our salmon for about 18 hours. At the conclusion of the smoking, the salmon should still appear to be raw, but it will feel drier and firmer.

Salmon is very sensitive to heat, so during the warmest summer days, we heat the sawdust in an exterior firebox so the smokehouse doesn't overheat. If the temperature rises too much, the outside of the salmon will cook and form a skin that prevents the smoke from flavoring and preserving the fish.

Salmon Bacon

2 pounds salmon belly (the
    fatty underside of the fish,
    available at most fish
    markets)
Coarse salt
¼ cup pure maple syrup

1. Rinse the salmon and pat it dry. Place it in a single layer in a flat container and cover it with coarse salt. Set it aside for 30 minutes.

2. Light a sawdust pile in a smokehouse or in an exterior firebox, at least 1 hour in advance.

3. Rinse the salt off under cold running water, and leave the salmon on a wire rack until dry to the touch, 20 to 50 minutes.

4. Coat the salmon with the maple syrup and allow to dry on a wire rack for about 15 minutes. Place the salmon in the smokehouse and smoke for about 18 hours, turning every 3 hours during the day.

Smoked Tuna Tenderloin

One 2- to 3-pound boneless
    tuna tenderloin
Coarse salt

Tuna can tolerate—and even benefits from—a higher level of heat than salmon. It also requires a long, continuous period of smoking. To accomplish this, we start with a fire in the exterior firebox and then continue with a fire in the smokehouse. This allows for a longer burn at a high enough temperature. This method is also good for swordfish, mahi mahi, wahoo, and shark.

1. Rinse the tuna and pat it dry. Place the fish in a flat container and cover it with the coarse salt. Set it aside for 2½ to 3 hours depending on the size of the tenderloin.

2. Rinse the salt off the tuna under cold running water and set it aside until dry to the touch.

3. Place at least 1½ feed sacks of dry sawdust inside the smokehouse and additional sawdust in the exterior firebox. Light the sawdust in the exterior chamber. Once it is smoldering,

place the tuna in the smokehouse. Before this sawdust burns out, light the sawdust pile inside the smokehouse. There should be enough sawdust to allow for a continuous burn for 36 hours. Turn the fish after the first 3 hours and then every 8 hours after that until done.

4. After 36 hours, remove the tuna from the smokehouse. The fish should have a little bit of a smoky cast. The flesh should be delicate and appear to be barely cooked—similar in appearance and texture to a finely smoked ham. Serve the smoked tuna thinly sliced.

Smoked Scallops

1 pound fresh scallops

Coarse salt

Smoked fresh scallops are delicate and sweet. They make a great appetizer, snack, or replacement for sausage in gumbos and soups. Scallops for smoking must be very fresh. They are very sensitive to heat, so on hot days, place the sawdust pile in the exterior firebox, not in the smokehouse.

1. Light a sawdust pile, in the smokehouse or in an exterior firebox, at least 1 hour in advance.

2. Rinse the scallops and pat them dry. Place them in a single layer in a flat container and cover them with the coarse salt. Set aside for 25 minutes.

3. Rinse the salt off under cold running water, and leave the scallops on a wire rack until dry to the touch.

4. Place the scallops in the smokehouse and smoke for 12 to 18 hours, turning them every 6 hours. This long period of smoking will not hurt the scallops as long as they are protected from excessive heat buildup.

Smoked Whole Trout

2 to 3 whole trout, dressed,
8 to 10 ounces each

Coarse salt

Like salmon, trout suffers with excess exposure to heat. If the temperature is too warm, the fat in the fish liquefies. When this happens, the flesh starts to separate, and a skin (pellicle) forms that prevents smoke from entering and flavoring or preserving the fish. This recipe can also be used for smaller mackerel and trout relatives.

1. Butterfly the fish, splaying it open along the spine, so that it sits flat (see photo on the next page). Place the butterflied trout in a large, flat container, cover with the coarse salt, and set aside for 1 hour.
2. Rinse the salt off and leave the trout on a wire rack until dry to the touch.
3. Meanwhile, light a sawdust pile in an exterior firebox at least 1 hour in advance.
4. Place the trout in the smokehouse, and smoke for at least 18 hours, turning them every 6 hours. If you continue smoking beyond this point, there is no need to continue turning the fish.

Smoked Haddock (Finnan Haddie)

2 to 3 large haddock fillets,
8 to 10 ounces each

Coarse salt

Soft and delicate in flavor, almost sweet, smoked haddock is golden, with slightly translucent but firm flesh. The smoked fish will last for ten to twelve days in the refrigerator. Smoked haddock is great in gumbos, stews, and chowders. In Nova Scotia, it is traditionally cooked in milk and then eaten as fillets.

1. Light a sawdust pile, in the smokehouse or in an exterior firebox, at least 1 hour in advance. Haddock is very sensitive to heat, so if the weather is hot, use the exterior firebox.

2. Rinse the haddock and pat it dry. Place the fillets in a single layer in a flat container and cover them with the coarse salt. Set aside for 30 minutes.

3. Rinse the salt off under cold running water, and leave the fillets on a wire rack until dry to the touch.

4. Place the haddock in the smokehouse, and smoke for at least 18 hours, turning them after the first 3 hours and then every 8 hours until they're done. As with scallops, longer smoking will not hurt the quality or flavor of the haddock.

Chapter nine

Suggested Menus

An Elegant Five-Course Creole Dinner

Similar to the dinners served every evening at Trout Point Lodge, all the courses here speak "Creole." This menu may take a little advance planning and preparation, but it will satisfy your most demanding guests.

CRAWFISH BISQUE - 69

SALMON CAKES - 118

MIXED GREEN SALAD WITH SUGARCANE VINAIGRETTE - 99

MARINATED SWORDFISH KEBABS - 120

LEMONGRASS CRÈME BRÛLÉE - 203

OR

CHOCOLATE GOURMANDISE - 200

An Easy-to-Prepare Creole Meal

For this four-course lunch or dinner, we've selected dishes that take only minutes each to prepare.

SCALLOPS EN BROCHETTE - 33

CREOLE CELERY ROOT SALAD - 87

PAELLA-JAMBALAYA - 150

APPLE TART - 196

An Elegant Creole Vegetarian Meal

The gourmet vegetarian will love this five-course feast with plenty of New Orleans flavor and style.

ROASTED EGGPLANT SOUP - 57
OR
CHILLED CREAM OF SWEET POTATO - 41

SHIITAKE MUSHROOMS ROCKEFELLER - 8
OR
WILD MUSHROOMS EN PAPILLOTE - 6

ENDIVE SALAD - 86

GUMBO DES HERBES - 135

OR

CREOLE-STYLE LOBSTER MUSHROOMS ETOUFFÉE - 104

PEACH CUSTARD TART - 196

OR

FLOURLESS CHOCOLATE ALMOND CAKE - 186

A Nova Scotia Seafood Feast

A diversity of fresh Nova Scotia seafood goes into this multicourse meal.

SHRIMP NOODLE SOUP - 62

SMOKED TROUT CAKES - 22

SEA BEAN AND MUSSEL SALAD - 92

GRILLED SHARK STEAKS WITH SAGE BUTTER SAUCE - 128

BLUEBERRY TART - 194

A Four-Course Vegetarian Lunch

The rich, full flavors of wild mushrooms, earthy sweet potatoes, and savory grilled eggplant make for incredible taste combinations without a hint of meat or seafood.

WILD MUSHROOM SOUP - 56

SWEET POTATO CAKES - 16

GRILLED EGGPLANT TART - 13

APRICOT TART - 192

Index

Chebogue Point, Nova Scotia, xxxi–xxxii
cheese:
    in artichoke and fresh herb salad, 88
    in grilled eggplant tart, 13–14
    for oysters Rockefeller, 36
    for quahogs Florentine on the half-shell, 34
    in salmon cakes, 118–19
    in shiitake mushrooms Rockefeller, 8–10
    in shrimp and green olive tart, 29
    in smoked salmon spaghetti alla carbonara, 122
    in Swiss chard and chestnut gratinée, 112–13
    in vegetable shepherd's pie, 106–7
    see also specific cheeses
cheesecakes:
    chocolate cherry, 182
    Trout Point, 182
Chef Prudhomme's Louisiana Kitchen (Prudhomme), xxx
cherry(ies), dried:
    in chocolate-cherry cheesecake, 182
    white chocolate, and almond bread pudding, 189
chestnut and Swiss chard gratinée, 112–13
chicken stock, 60
chili, cashew, 52–53
Chinese noodles and shrimp soup, 62
chocolate:
    -almond cake, flourless, with white and dark ganache, 186–87
    -cherry cheesecake, 182
    gourmandise, 200
    pineapple mint, mousse, 184
    see also white chocolate
chowder, smoked salmon, 64–65
ciabatta, rosemary, 171–72
clafoutis, wild blackberry breakfast, 82
clams:
    casserole of cherrystones, artichokes, and thyme, 131–32
    in pâté à la rapure (rappie pie), 158–59
    quahogs Florentine on the half-shell, 34
clementine and black olive salad, 86–87
coconut:
    ice cream, 204–5
    milk, in roasted eggplant soup, 57
    milk, in saffron mussel bisque, 58, 60
Commander's Palace, xxx
Cooper, Sister Mary Ursula, xxxi
cornmeal:
    -crusted oyster mushrooms, 11
    -crusted scallops with wild sweet fern butter, spicy, 129

    in herb garden bread, 175–76
    sun-dried tomato bread with white, 174
courtbouillon, perch and hake, 142–43
crawfish:
    bisque, 69
    and carrot jambalaya, 148
cream cheese:
    in chocolate-cherry cheesecake, 182
    in Trout Point cheesecake, 182
crème anglaise, wintergreen, 83
crème brûlée:
    lemongrass, 203
    maple, 202
crème fraîche:
    basic, 47
    bullrush blinis topped with salmon, Beluga caviar and, 77
    in sole in wile sorrel velouté sauce, 79–80
Creole, Creole-style:
    celery root salad, 87
    cooking traditions, xxviii–xxx, 3, 39, 101–2, 134, 139–40, 152
    lobster mushrooms étouffée, 104
    red beans and rice, 111
    seasoning mixes, 37
    shrimp, 146–47
    stuffed bell peppers, 108
    stuffed eggplants, 109–10
    suggested menus, 217–18, 220–21
cucumber, for tuna tartare, 20–21
custard tarts:
    peach, 196–97
    wild blackberry, 181

daube, tuna, 156–57
David, Elizabeth, 86
desserts, 179–205
    apple tart, 194–95
    apricot tart, 192
    basic short dough for pie and tart crusts, 180–81
    blueberry bread pudding, 188
    blueberry tart, 194
    chocolate cherry cheesecake, 182
    chocolate gourmandise, 200
    coconut ice cream, 204–5
    dried cherry, white chocolate, and almond bread pudding, 189
    flourless chocolate almond cake with white and dark chocolate ganache, 186–87
    lemongrass crème brûlée, 203

About the Authors

Daniel Abel grew up in Lafayette, Louisiana, center of Acadian culture. His grandparents were farmers who homesteaded in southern Louisiana, eventually becoming hotel owners and restaurateurs. As a student he worked at the renowned Thelma's restaurant in Breaux Bridge, and later became manager of jazz musician Al Hirt's Café St. Cécile. He and his partners established Chicory Farm, where they made cheese from the milk of their own goats and sheep, cultivated mushrooms, and grew specialty produce. Mr. Abel also worked as the executive chef and manager of the critically acclaimed Creole restaurant Chicory Farm Café in New Orleans, and has taught cooking lessons in Louisiana and Canada. He is the coauthor of a book on children and gun safety and is the author of several legal treatises.

Vaughn Perret was born and raised in New Orleans, attending Loyola and Tulane universities for studies in history and anthropology before entering Cornell University Law School. An avid food lover, traveler, and expert on wild edibles, Mr. Perret has eaten his way through Western Europe, North Africa, and Asia since his college days, at one time living in Paris. He shares chef duties at Trout Point Lodge and the Inn at Coyote Mountain and was the principal investigator for a U.S. Department of Agriculture research project on gourmet mushrooms. A master gardener, he has established organic farms in Louisiana, Canada, and Costa Rica, and has acted as an adviser to countless New Orleans chefs on food ingredients.

Charles Leary is a one-time Chinese history professor turned cheesemaker, baker, and chef. After earning degrees from Kenyon College and Cornell University, Dr. Leary made accolade-winning, European-style cheeses in Louisiana and Nova Scotia for ten years. He then focused on cooking and helped establish the Nova Scotia Seafood Cooking School at Trout Point Lodge and the Tropical Creole Cooking School in Costa Rica. A specialist in desserts, pastries, and breads, he has recently begun experimenting with the culinary uses of tropical fruits while cooking at the Inn at Coyote Mountain. He has written articles for a wide variety of publications, from the New Orleans *Times-Picayune* to the *Dairy Goat Journal*.

Daniel Abel, Vaughn Perret, and Charles Leary now split their time between Nova Scotia, Louisiana, Spain, and Costa Rica. Among only a handful of North Americans to claim the honor, Abel, Perret, and Leary were inducted into the prestigious French Cheesemakers Guild in 1994. They also won the Tibbets Award from the U.S. Small Business Administration, a national honor. They are members of the International Association of Culinary Professionals, and their accomplishments as farmers, innkeepers, and chefs have been praised by *The New York Times, Food & Wine, Travel & Leisure,* and the Food Network. Their recipes have been published in a variety of places, including *Harrowsmith Country Life, Food & Wine,* and *Louisiana Cookin'.* Jamie Shannon, the former longtime executive chef of Commander's Palace restaurant in New Orleans said, "Every time I talk to them, I learn something."

About the Type

This book is set in Albertina, a typeface designed in the 1960s by Charles Brand based on the principles of calligraphy. Typesetting machines of the period were unable to reproduce the spacing of cursive type; but the Albertina design found new life with digital type technology. Frank E. Blokland, of the Dutch Type Library, worked with him to develop a digital version of Albertina that captures the full grace and style of Brand's original drawings.